Claire Macdonald and her husband run Kinloch Lodge Hotel on the Isle of Skye, which is also the family home for them and their four children. Claire is a well-known exponent of Scottish cooking and travels widely, lecturing and demonstrating recipes.

Also by Claire Macdonald

SEASONAL COOKING
SWEET THINGS
MORE SEASONAL COOKING
CELEBRATIONS
LUNCHES

and published by Corgi Books

Claire
Macdonald

OF MACDONALD

Suppers

CORGI BOOKS

SUPPERS
A CORGI BOOK : 0 552 14209 3

Originally published in Great Britain by Doubleday,
a division of Transworld Publishers

PRINTING HISTORY
Doubleday edition published 1994
Corgi edition published 1996

5 7 9 10 8 6 4

Set in Baskerville by
Hewer Text Composition Services, Edinburgh.

Corgi Books are published by Transworld Publishers,
61–63 Uxbridge Road, London W5 5SA,
a division of The Random House Group Ltd,
in Australia by Random House Australia (Pty) Ltd,
20 Alfred Street, Milsons Point, Sydney, NSW 2061, Australia,
in New Zealand by Random House New Zealand Ltd,
18 Poland Road, Glenfield, Auckland 10, New Zealand
and in South Africa by Random House (Pty) Ltd,
Endulini, 5a Jubilee Road, Parktown 2193, South Africa.

Printed and bound in Great Britain by
Cox & Wyman Ltd, Reading, Berkshire.

To my dearest friend Minty

ACKNOWLEDGEMENTS

Thank you and love to Godfrey, Isabella, Meriel and Hugo; to everyone at Bantam Press, especially Sally Gaminara; to all my friends, but especially Minty and my sisters Camilla and Olivia.

Suppers

Contents

Introduction

It is my experience that it is not only in this household that the cry goes up daily 'Whatever shall we have for supper?' No sooner have I said it than I regret it, because when you have four children as we do, you are bound to get, as I do, four different answers. And therein lies a potential pitfall – to cook à la carte for your family, in an effort to please them all. This is just not on. If they all have to eat food which wouldn't be their choice, they will soon learn to like it; if they are hungry enough they will eat anything, and the most important person in the providing of food in a family is you, the cook.

In an effort to make the daily cooking fun, I found way back that I need a variety of ingredients and a wide and differing range of types of food, ranging from ethnic to bangers and mash. This necessitates children learning from an early age to like not only mundane things such as mushrooms, tomatoes and cheese (blue as well as Cheddar, goats' as well as cows') but also things like fresh ginger and garlic, curry and fish and shellfish This gives you, the cook, variety, which means fun. I can think of nothing more deadly than having a small repertoire of dishes which the family will eat, Even if I can never think of a single thing to give them, once inspired, I'm away!

This is where this book is intended to be helpful to you. To give you the ideas for supper food, informal food for every day, for special occasions, for when you have people staying and want to make just that bit more effort than is required by the usual everyday one-course meal which, followed by fruit, is what supper generally consists of for us. There is a chapter on suggestions for supper on Sundays, when somehow we, as well as countless other families, have a simple supper because it is the one day of the week when we have a large lunch – a reversal to how we eat on the other six days of the week.

There is a chapter on using up leftover food, and panic suppers which can be made from a few items in your storecupboard or fast thawable food from your freezer. There is a chapter on suppers for children, which contains dishes greatly enjoyed by our children as they have grown up, and which seem to appeal to their friends, as well as some which children themselves can make. There is a small chapter with a few suggestions for quick first courses, which can go before the dishes in 'More than Just the Family' or 'Special Occasions'. The latter are intended for times when a certain celebration is in order, like birthdays, anniversaries, end of school or university term times – all homecomings are special occasions for us.

But the usual is the everyday supper. These days I feel that families eat more informally as a rule. Fewer people use dining rooms (if indeed they have one) on a daily basis, using their kitchen as a dining room for the most part. This has changed the appearance of many kitchens. They are no longer the utilitarian rooms they used to be, but have become far, far more attractive. The wide choice of kitchen furniture available ranges from the very reasonably priced to the hand-crafted and very expensive, but it is all designed to make the kitchen much more of a living room than a working room. I am all in favour of this, because I feel that I am missing out if I am working in the kitchen whilst everyone else is next door! I think a kitchen should be a sociable room, which these days it is, ever increasingly.

There is a temptation to buy ready-cooked food. I have to say that when Godfrey does the weekly shop at the Cash and Carry in Inverness he gets us something for supper at Marks & Spencer, whose range of ready-cooked foods is extensive. I often wonder if I would buy food ready cooked more often if I lived nearer to Marks & Spencer, but I hope I wouldn't. I think that there is nothing better than cooking, except eating the food you've cooked around a table with family and friends – feeding people is one of the most satisfying experiences. Supper-time is a sociable time, and a time for catching up on the day's events, and just generally communicating. Much as I love the occasional ready-cooked dish from M & S, there is no getting away from the fact that, good though most of these are, the manufacturers have to play safe with the seasonings, and so nothing has quite the impact of flavour that I would like. This is really only obtainable by making your own food.

On this note, I must say that in all the recipes in this book the seasonings are guidelines, because taste is such a personal thing.

No-one can dictate to you how much salt you should like – some people like none, or a very small amount, whilst some – us, I regret to say – love salt. That is why in many of the recipes you will see 1–2 cloves of garlic. Some people (me, for example, and the rest of our family I am thankful to say!) like garlic to a far greater extent than others, so just use one clove if you like a less pronounced taste. The same must be said about pepper. We love lots of pepper, a greatly underrated spice in my opinion. I do feel that those who grind a pepper mill a couple of times don't give pepper the chance it deserves in a recipe – such a small amount would be hardly noticeable. But just how much you add to the ingredients must depend on your own taste.

I love suppers which are meals in one dish, perhaps needing only an accompanying salad. This book is full of such recipes – Smoked Haddock Roulade, for example, or Cheese, Ham and Mushroom Puff Pastry Slice, to give just two examples. And then there is the stew and casserole type of dish, which tastes much better when made in advance and reheated before supper-time – these dishes are so convenient. Any food which isn't last-minute is a boon. There are other dishes for which all the preparation can be done well in advance, and which take literally minutes to cook – the stir-fry recipes fall into this category, needing only boiled Basmati rice and perhaps a salad to go with them.

Long since gone are the days of the meat and two veg type of meal – when we were first married (golly, twenty-five years ago!) I never felt that I was feeding Godfrey properly if supper didn't include meat or fish. And yet we, as well as so many families in Britain today, eat meat far less frequently than we used to. This doesn't mean that we like meat any the less, we love beef, lamb, chicken and pork, but we just eat it far less often. Suppers very often consist of vegetables-based food, with a great deal of pasta and rice, both of which are family favourites. You will find several different recipes for risottos within this book – risotto, with whatever ingredients, is a top favourite supper request, and a unanimous one.

I really hope that if you, like me, are perpetually wondering what to have for supper, you will find help in this book. And that you will enjoy the results!

Suppers for Singles

Baked Chicken with Red Onions

Sautéed Chicken with Globe Artichokes

Baked Lamb with Tomatoes, Garlic and Mushrooms

Pheasant Breast with Orange and Chestnuts

Baked Fillets of Plaice with White Wine and Shallots

Oysters Benedict

Smoked Salmon and Egg Salad with Dill Dressing

Creamy Chicken and Tarragon Mousse

Sautéed Plaice Fillets with Parsley and Lemon Juice

Pasta with Stilton and Walnuts

SUPPER FOR SINGLES

I am not really in a position to speak about cooking for myself and no-one else. There are the occasional nights when Godfrey is away and for supper on these occasions I eat what I like best and what is easiest to prepare, which for me is granary bread toasted and spread with butter and marmite, with grilled tomatoes. But I often imagine, or try to, just what it would feel like to have only me to cook for permanently, with the occasional exception when I would have people to stay, or have a dinner party. These imaginings are usually prompted by requests for some ideas on catering for people living by themselves.

If it were for me, I would try to keep to the forefront of my mind the fact that I am important, to me at any rate! – and that I deserve a good supper each day, eaten at a set table, accompanied by wine. Just because I am alone doesn't mean that I would feel any guilt about planning, shopping and cooking dishes which involve thought and time in their conception, preparation and cooking.

So often I hear the same remark from people living by themselves (which sounds so much less bleak than saying living alone) to the effect that it isn't really worth cooking just for yourself. It jolly well is! So I think the important thing is to start by dispensing with that myth.

And then I'm sure people think in terms of a chop or two, a chicken portion, and for special occasions or at a weekend, perhaps a steak. Well, obviously all these items have their place in the dishes we will eat, but life for the single person contains a far wider culinary perspective than that. I quite realize that no one wants to make a dish for four people and then eat it on four consecutive days, but with a freezer there is no need for that. Most of the recipes in the other chapters in this book could be made in half quantities, and the rest of the dish, uneaten at the first supper, could be frozen and eaten at supper on a day when time for cooking is short. This is economical as well as being convenient.

I realize that people living by themselves are in widely differing circumstances. There are those who are busy men or women, out most days working and therefore with little time for cooking, and there are those who do not work, who are retired, who may be supposed to have more time on their hands, although it is my experience that, for the most part, these people are often the busiest if they do voluntary work.

Never be afraid to ask in shops for small amounts – I heard just today of a recently widowed grandmother who buys more than she can eat herself, because she feels embarrassed to ask for just two rashers of bacon, for example. Shops should be, and most are, glad to sell anything, however small in quantity.

So do look through the other chapters in this book, and adapt the recipes in quantity to your own appetite. And never forget that you are indeed most worthwhile to cook for!

Baked Chicken with Red Onions

I never think we use red onions enough in our cooking. They are milder than ordinary onions, and have a delicious flavour. In this recipe, the onions are cooked for about 45 minutes so that they caramelize, and the chicken is then pushed down amongst the onions to cook.

---

3 red onions
1 tbsp sunflower oil + ½ oz/
*   14 g butter*
Salt and freshly ground
*   black pepper*

A pinch of sugar
¼ pt/140 ml dry sherry
1 large chicken joint

Skin the onions and slice them finely. Heat the oil and melt the butter together in a casserole and cook the onions, stirring occasionally to prevent them from sticking. Season with the salt, pepper and sugar. After 20 minutes' cooking, pour in the sherry. Continue to cook for a further 20–25 minutes, then push the chicken piece down into the onions, spooning the onions on top.

Cover the casserole with a lid, and bake in a moderate oven, 350°F/180°C/Gas Mark 4, for 20 minutes. Test to see if the chicken is cooked by pushing a knife into the thickest part of the chicken. The juices should run clear. If they are even faintly tinged with pink, give the casserole a further few minutes in the oven.

I like to eat this with creamily mashed potatoes and a green vegetable such as courgettes, broccoli, or cabbage.

Sautéed Chicken with Globe Artichokes

This is a dish which is a treat to eat. Although you can make it with tinned artichoke bottoms (drain off their brine and rinse them well under running cold water), it is much nicer made with fresh artichokes. I like to eat it with either new or mashed potatoes, and a salad.

---

2 globe artichokes
1 oz/28 g butter and 1 tbsp
  sunflower oil
1 tsp flour
1 chicken joint (breast,
  leg, whatever you
  choose)
1 clove of garlic, skinned
  and finely chopped

¼ pt/140 ml dry white
  wine
1 egg yolk
2 tbsp double cream
½ tsp cornflour
Salt and ground black
  pepper

Cut the artichokes in quarters, cutting downwards. Cut away the tough outer leaves, and pull out the chokes. Cut off the stems about ½ in/1 cm below the artichokes' bases. Melt the butter and heat the oil together in a casserole. Rub the flour into the chicken and brown it on each side in the hot butter and oil. Then add the chopped garlic and the pieces of trimmed artichoke to the chicken in the casserole. Pour in the wine.

Cook the casserole in a moderate oven, 350°F/180°C/Gas Mark 4, for 15 minutes. Stick a knife into the thickest part of the chicken. If the juices run clear, it is cooked. Stick the knife into a piece of artichoke to test for tenderness. If either needs more cooking, put the casserole back in the oven for a further few minutes.

Meanwhile, mix together the egg yolk, cream and cornflour. When the chicken is cooked, take the dish out of the oven, mix a little of the hot juices into the creamy mixture, then stir this into the juices in the casserole. Stir over very low heat till it thickens. Season with salt and pepper to your taste.

Baked Lamb with Tomatoes, Garlic and Mushrooms

Depending how you feel, you can make this using either lamb chops or noisettes of lamb. If you don't like garlic, just leave it out.

I like this with baked potatoes, and cauliflower dusted with fried breadcrumbs and parsley.

---

2 tbsp olive oil
2 noisettes of lamb, or 2 lamb chops
1 onion, skinned and finely sliced
1 clove of garlic, skinned and finely chopped
2 oz/56 g mushrooms, wiped and chopped – stalks trimmed but not pulled out
2 tomatoes, each dipped in boiling water on the end of a fork then skinned; cut each in half, scoop away the seeds and chop the flesh
¼ pt/140 ml dry white wine
Salt and ground black pepper

Heat the oil in a casserole and brown the lamb on each side. Remove to a warm dish. Put the sliced onion into the casserole and cook it till it is soft and transparent-looking, and just beginning to turn golden. Then add the garlic and the mushrooms. Cook till the mushrooms are well done. Stir in the chopped tomatoes and the wine and add salt and pepper. Replace the lamb in the casserole.

Cover with a lid, and bake in moderate oven, 350°F/180°C/Gas Mark 4, for 15 minutes. This dish can be made ahead and kept, when cooled, in the fridge. To reheat, take the dish into room temperature for an hour before reheating. Simmer over gentle heat for 10 minutes.

Pheasant Breast with Orange and Chestnuts

From about December onwards it is possible to buy pheasant breasts in butchers' shops and most supermarkets. They do shrink as they cook, so if they look small, buy two. This recipe combines the pheasant with the complementary flavours of orange and chestnuts. To save opening a tin of whole chestnuts and freezing what you don't use, buy fresh chestnuts and boil them for 10 minutes. They should then be ready to have their skins nicked and cut off. They taste much nicer than tinned ones!

Serve this casserole with mashed potatoes and with finely sliced cabbage stir-fried with grainy mustard.

1 or 2 pheasant breasts
1 tbsp flour mixed with salt and ground black pepper
2 tbsp sunflower oil
1 onion, skinned and chopped
¼ pt/140 ml red wine, or stock if you prefer

About 6 chestnuts, shelled and chopped
1 orange, peel cut off with a serrated knife, and flesh chopped
Salt and ground black pepper

Coat the pheasant breasts in the seasoned flour. Heat the oil in a casserole dish, and brown the pheasant breasts on each side. Remove them to a warm dish. Add the chopped onion to the casserole and cook for a few minutes, till the onion is soft. Stir in the red wine or stock, the chopped chestnuts and the chopped orange. Replace the pheasant breasts in the casserole.

Cover with a lid and bake in a moderate oven, 350°F/180°C/Gas Mark 4, for 20 minutes. Take out of the oven, season with salt and pepper, and eat as soon as you can.

Baked Fillets of Plaice with White Wine and Shallots

Lemon sole is more fashionable than plaice, but I far prefer to eat plaice. I think the flavour of plaice is so good, whereas lemon sole has little flavour by comparison.

I like to eat this with spinach, steamed till it just wilts and seasoned with a grating of nutmeg and with plenty of butter chopped into it, and with new or mashed potatoes.

---

3 shallots, very finely chopped
¼ pt/140 ml dry white wine
A pinch of salt and a grinding of black pepper

2 or 3 filleted plaice – depending on your appetite and the size of the fish

---

Put the finely chopped shallots and the wine, salt and pepper into a saucepan over moderate heat, and simmer till the wine has reduced away to virtually nothing. Put the fillets of plaice into a buttered ovenproof dish, and spoon the cooked onion mixture on top, spreading it over the fish.

Cover the dish, and bake in a moderate oven, 350°F/180°C/Gas Mark 4, for 10–15 minutes.

Oysters Benedict

Delicious farmed oysters are ever easier to buy, and in this dish oysters are substituted for poached eggs in a variation on the classic Benedict dish. Most fish and all shellfish go very well with ham and bacon, and the slice of ham under the oysters and on top of the toasted muffin makes for a perfect supper dish. With the hollandaise sauce, this is a far nicer combination for my taste than the version with eggs.

A green salad is the only accompaniment necessary.

---

1 muffin, split and toasted
2 slices of roast ham,
trimmed of any fat
6–12 shelled oysters,
depending on your
appetite
1 oz/28 g butter – for
cooking the oysters
briefly

For the hollandaise sauce:
3 tbsp wine vinegar (white
or red)
1 tsp peppercorns
1–2 crushed parsley stalks
1 slice of onion (raw)
2 egg yolks
3 oz/84 g butter

To make the sauce, put the vinegar, peppercorns, parsley stalks and onion slice into a small saucepan and reduce the vinegar by half. This will take a very short time, so take care not to let it boil dry. In a pyrex bowl, beat the egg yolks with the strained reduced vinegar. Put the bowl over a pan of gently simmering water, and beat in the butter, a small piece at a time. When the butter is all incorporated and you have a thick glossy sauce, take the bowl off the heat. Meanwhile melt the 1 oz/28 g butter in a frying pan and briefly cook the oysters.

Put the toasted muffin halves on a warmed serving plate, cover them with the ham, and divide the oysters between the halved muffins. Spoon the hollandaise over each muffin with its covering, and eat immediately.

Smoked Salmon and
Egg Salad with Dill Dressing

One of the advantages of living by oneself is surely that eating can consist of treats which are out of the question for numbers of people living together – treats on an almost daily basis, that is! This makes a really good salad for supper on a hot summer evening, and it can be prepared almost entirely in advance, needing only to be assembled before being enjoyed, with a glass of chilled white wine and a plate of buttered granary bread.

Crisp lettuce leaves, of whatever assortment you like
2 oz/56 g smoked salmon
2 hardboiled eggs, shelled and chopped

About 6 cherry tomatoes, halved
For the dressing:
1 tbsp chopped dill weed
2 tbsp fromage frais
1 tsp mayonnaise
Ground black pepper

Arrange the lettuce leaves on a serving plate. Chop the smoked salmon, mix well with the chopped hardboiled eggs, and pile this mixture and the halved cherry tomatoes in the middle of the plate.

For the dressing, mix together the chopped dill weed, the fromage frais, mayonnaise and black pepper, and spoon over the entire salad.

Creamy Chicken and Tarragon Mousse

This is a perfect supper for a summer evening. You can prepare it entirely the previous day, so that all you need to do is to turn it out on a few lettuce leaves. If you like, you can serve it with a fromage frais or mayonnaise based sauce – as in the recipe for Smoked Salmon and Egg salad.

1 chicken breast	*A few tarragon leaves*
½ pt/285 ml chicken stock,	*A stick of celery – optional*
made with water and a	*1 tsp gelatine*
Kallo stock cube – they	*3–4 tarragon leaves,*
contain no additives and	*chopped*
are very much better than	*2 tbsp whipped cream*
the other stock cube	*A pinch of salt*
makes	*Freshly ground black*
A slice of raw onion	*pepper*
	A dash of Tabasco sauce

Put the chicken breast into a saucepan with the stock, the onion, tarragon leaves and celery. Poach very gently till the chicken is cooked – about 10–15 minutes. Stick a knife into the chicken to see if the juices run clear. If they are tinged with pink, simmer for another few minutes. Let the chicken cool in the stock – this keeps it moist.

Drain ¼ pint/140 ml of stock into a small saucepan and heat. Sprinkle in the teaspoonful of gelatine, and stir till it dissolves completely. Cool.

Put the chicken, cut in bits, into a food processor with the tarragon leaves. Whiz, adding the cooled gelatine in the stock. Whiz in the whipped cream, the salt, pepper and Tabasco, and scrape this mixture into a bowl to set. Leave for several hours, with the bowl covered, in the fridge, or make the day before and leave overnight.

Sautéed Plaice Fillets
with Parsley and Lemon Juice

This takes about 4 minutes to cook. The parsley can be chopped in advance. It is one of the nicest ways to eat fish – I buy filleted plaice, but you could use any white fish for this. If you use cod, or any thicker fleshed fish than plaice or lemon sole for example, you will need a minute or so longer cooking time.

This is good with a vegetable like courgettes cooked with garlic, or steamed broccoli, and creamily mashed potatoes.

---

2 or 3 filleted plaice, depending on their size and your appetite	*1 oz/28 g butter + 2 tsp sunflower oil*
1 tbsp flour sieved on to a plate with a little salt	*1 oz/28 g butter*
	2 tsp lemon juice
	Ground black pepper
	1 tbsp finely chopped parsley

Dip the fish in the sieved flour, on each side. Melt 1 oz/28 g of butter and heat the sunflower oil in a frying pan and cook the fish – it will take less than a minute each side. Dish them on to a warmed serving plate and add the other piece of butter to the frying pan, with the lemon juice, pepper and chopped parsley. Let it bubble briefly, then pour this over the cooked fish on your plate. Serve immediately.

Pasta with Stilton and Walnuts

Any of the pasta recipes in other chapters are useful and usable for single people, if the quantities are scaled down according to appetite. This recipe is quick and simple to make, and combines the creamy sharpness of the Stilton (you can substitute any other type of blue cheese with the exception of Danish Blue, which has all the sharpness but none of the creaminess) with the crunch of the walnuts. It really is worthwhile dry-frying the chopped walnuts first, because it freshens up their taste no end. All nuts tend to become stale as they sit on our shelves, no matter how airtight their containers, but I think walnuts deteriorate much more noticeably than others. The sliced leeks are perfect, tastewise, with both the walnuts and the Stilton. Use any shape of pasta you like, and I like to eat a green salad with this.

About 3 oz/84 g pasta, fresh or dried, boiled in plenty of salty water till you can push your – clean – thumbnail into a bit; beware overcooking, which renders pasta slimy

1 tbsp olive oil

1 medium leek, washed, trimmed and thinly sliced

1 clove of garlic, skinned and very finely chopped

2 oz/56 g walnuts, chopped and dry-fried in a saucepan for about 5 mins

Freshly ground black pepper

2–3 oz/56–84 g Stilton, crumbled

Heat the oil and cook the sliced leek and the garlic till the leek is quite soft – about 3–4 minutes. Add the chopped walnuts and the pepper. Mix this into the drained cooked pasta with the crumbled Stilton and eat immediately.

First Courses

Egg, Cucumber and Dill Mousse

*Cheese Pastry Tartlets with Tomato and
Garlic Mayonnaise and Quails' Eggs*

Deep-Fried Mushrooms in a Garlic and Slightly Curried Batter

Anchovy Puffs

Parmesan Toasts

Artichoke Heart, Quails' Egg and Smoked Salmon Salad

Warm Chicken Liver Salad

Cucumber and Dill Soup

Herb and Mushroom Crêpes

Asparagus Salad

FIRST COURSES

These recipes can be combined with those in the chapter which follows, 'More than Just the Family', or the one on 'Special Occasions' towards the end of the book. With the exception of Deep-Fried Mushrooms, everything described here can be made in advance.

Egg, Cucumber and Dill Mousse

This mousse has two different textures, the grated cucumber and the chopped eggs. It is a sumptuous mousse, and makes a perfect main course on warm summer evenings as well as an ideal first course when you have guests.

SERVES 6–8

1 cucumber, not peeled, grated and sprinkled with a little salt and left to sit for half an hour – the juices which collect must be drained away	6 tbsp mayonnaise
	½ pt/285 ml creamy fromage frais (as opposed to the low fat kind)
8 hardboiled eggs, shelled and chopped	1 tbsp white wine vinegar
	1 tsp sugar
¼ pt/140 ml chicken stock with 1 sachet of gelatine sprinkled in and dissolved over gentle heat	1 large handful dill weed, chopped
	2 tbsp snipped chives

When the stock and gelatine mixture has cooled completely, stir it into the mayonnaise and add the chopped eggs and the drained grated cucumber. Fold in the fromage frais, the wine vinegar, sugar, chopped dill weed and chives and put this mixture into a glass or china serving dish, having first tasted to see if there is enough seasoning for your liking. If not, just add a bit more salt and some freshly ground black pepper.

Cheese Pastry Tartlets with Tomato and Garlic Mayonnaise and Quails' Eggs

This is a new first course for us here at Kinloch this year, and it is so good, with a little salad at the side of the plate, and two tartlets per person. You can make the mayonnaise in the morning for supper that night, and the cheese tartlets, too, can be made in the morning. All you need to do before supper is to assemble everything.

SERVES 6

18 quails' eggs, boiled for 4 minutes

For the pastry:

3 oz/85 g butter, hard from the fridge, cut into bits in a processor

6 oz/170 g plain flour

1 tsp (2 tsp) mustard powder

2 oz/56 g Cheddar cheese, grated

A dash of Tabasco sauce

For the mayonnaise:

1 whole egg + 1 yolk

½ tsp salt

1 tsp sugar

Lots of ground black pepper

1 tsp English mustard

1 clove of garlic, skinned and finely chopped

½ pt/285 ml olive oil, or if you prefer, half and half olive and sunflower oils

1–2 tbsp wine vinegar

6 tomatoes

Whiz all the ingredients for the pastry in a food processor, adding just enough cold water to bind them together. Roll the pastry out on a floured surface and cut twelve circles to fit individual places in a (preferably non-stick) small cake or jam tart tin. These usually have twelve places to a tin. Put a circle in each place, pressing them gently down to fit.

Put the tins in the fridge for half an hour, then bake in a moderately hot oven, 350°F/180°C/Gas Mark 4, till they are pale golden, about 12–15 minutes. Slip them on to a wire cooling rack.

To make the mayonnaise, whiz the whole egg and yolk, salt, sugar, pepper, mustard and garlic in the processor, then very gradually, drop by drop at first, then in a thin trickle, add the oil. Next whiz in 1 tablespoon of the wine vinegar, taste, and if you like a sharper mayonnaise add the second spoonful.

Skin the tomatoes by dipping them in boiling water, speared on the end of a fork, or alternatively by pouring boiling water over them in a bowl and stabbing each with a knife. After about 30 seconds, pour the water off, and the skins should slip easily off the tomatoes. Cut them in half, then in quarters, and scoop away the seeds. Chop the flesh into fine dice. Mix it into the mayonnaise.

Before serving, shell the quails' eggs, and cut each one in half. Put the pastry tartlets on to serving plates, two to each plate, and put a good spoonful of mayonnaise into each, then arrange three halves of egg on top. Put a small amount of salad leaves at the side of the tartlets.

Deep-Fried Mushrooms in a Garlic and Slightly Curried Batter

This batter differs from all the very many other recipes I've tried over the years in that it stays crisp. In all other cases the mushrooms, once deep-fried, turn flabby, very disappointingly. These are quite filling, so don't feel mean if you allow three average-sized mushrooms per person. You can, if you like, serve a garlic mayonnaise as an accompanying sauce, but I think it is rather gilding the lily.

18 even-sized medium mushrooms, stalks cut level with the caps but not pulled out altogether (if possible)	*1 large clove of garlic, skinned and very finely chopped*
For the batter:	*8 oz/225 g plain flour sieved into a bowl*
½ tsp salt	*½ pt/285 ml milk*
1 tsp medium curry powder	*2 tsp bicarbonate of soda*
	Sunflower oil for deep-frying

Mix the salt, curry powder and chopped garlic into the flour and, using a flat wire whisk, gradually mix in the milk. Do this, if it is more convenient, in the morning, ready for supper that evening. Just before you want to start deep-frying, sieve the bicarbonate of soda into the mixture – it will go slightly frothy. Mix it in well. Dip each mushroom in the batter, then put them straight into the hot fat. Test the fat to see if it's hot enough by dropping a cube of bread in; if it sizzles, it's ready for the mushrooms. Cook them till they turn golden brown all over, pick them out with a slotted spoon and put them on a heatproof dish lined with several thicknesses of absorbent kitchen paper. Serve as soon as possible.

Anchovy Puffs

These are so good, and they can be served with drinks, as a sort of cross between a canapé and a first course eaten with the fingers. The crunch of the nuts contrasts well with the smooth biscuity pastry. If you have any trouble finding pecan nuts, substitute walnuts.

3 oz/84 g butter	*4 oz/112 g chopped pecan*
3 oz/84 g cream cheese, such	*nuts*
as Philadelphia	*1 tube anchovy paste – or*
6 oz/170 g plain flour	*Gentleman's Relish*

Mix together the butter and cream cheese, gradually working in the flour. Put the pastry into the fridge for half an hour, then roll it out as thinly as possible, on a floured surface, and cut into small circles with a biscuit cutter. Spread each circle with a little of the anchovy paste. Put a few chopped pecan nuts on each, and fold each circle in half, to form a semi-circle. Put the semi-circles on a lightly greased baking sheet and bake in 400°F/200°C/Gas Mark 6 oven for 7–10 minutes. Serve warm.

Parmesan Toasts

These, like the Anchovy Puffs, are meant to be eaten with drinks before supper. If the thought of cooking with mayonnaise sounds a bit odd to you, don't be put off, they are delicious. You can make the croûtons a day in advance, and just spread them with the Parmesan mixture and grill them before you want to serve them.

ENOUGH FOR 6

3 oz/84 g butter	*2 spring onions, trimmed*
6 slices of bread	*and finely chopped*
6 oz/170 g fresh Parmesan	*A pinch of salt and plenty of*
cheese, grated	*freshly ground black*
1 tbsp mayonnaise	*pepper*

Melt the butter and brush each slice of bread with it, brushing on each side. Cut circles out of each slice with a small biscuit cutter and put them on a baking tray. Toast them, turning them over so they cook on each side.

Before your guests arrive, spread each circle with the Parmesan well mixed with the mayonnaise, finely chopped spring onions, salt and pepper. Put the circles back on the baking tray and pop them under a hot grill till they are slightly puffed up and golden brown. These are good eaten cooled, but much the nicest served hot!

Artichoke Heart, Quails' Egg and Smoked Salmon Salad

Salads with strong individual characters, as it were, as their components, make my favourite first courses. They are convenient in that they can be prepared well in advance, only needing to be assembled before supper-time. In this salad the tastes of the artichoke hearts (well drained of their brine), the quails' eggs and the smoked salmon all complement each other.

SERVES 6

Mixed salad greens	*12 oz/340 g thinly sliced*
2–3 artichoke hearts per	* smoked salmon*
* person*	*2 tbsp finely chopped*
18 quails' eggs, boiled for 4	* parsley and snipped*
* minutes*	* chives, mixed*
	French dressing

On six serving plates distribute the salad greenery. On top arrange the artichoke hearts, each cut in half, the shelled and halved quails' eggs and the smoked salmon, cut into thin strips. Scatter the parsley and chives over the surface of each, and hand around the French dressing in a jug with a spoon for serving, so that guests can help themselves as they like – some, or none at all.

Warm Chicken Liver Salad

This is so good – the other parts of this salad are tiny cubes of bread, shallow-fried in butter and oil (the oil prevents the butter from burning), and small bits of crisply cooked bacon, preferably smoked bacon. If you make a French dressing with grainy mustard, stirring it in well, it seems to enhance the flavours of this first course salad.

SERVES 6

4 oz/112 g butter + 4 tbsp sunflower oil
3 slices of bread, crusts cut off and bread cut into cubes as small as possible
6 slices of smoked streaky bacon, grilled till crisp, then broken into small bits

1½ lb/675 g chicken livers
Assorted salad greenery
2 tbsp finely chopped parsley and snipped chives, mixed
French dressing made with 1 tsp grainy mustard

In the morning you can make the croûtons and grill the bacon – both will reheat before supper. Melt 2 oz/56 g of the butter and heat 2 tablespoons of the oil in a frying pan and fry the bread cubes, turning them continually to prevent them from burning, and cooking them till they are golden brown. As they cook, scoop them on to a plate with two or three thicknesses of kitchen paper, to absorb excess grease. Pick over the chicken livers, removing any unpleasant bits and chopping any large bits of liver.

Before serving, arrange the salad greens on six plates. Melt the rest of the butter and heat the remaining oil in a frying pan and when they are hot, add the prepared chicken livers. Cook them till they are sealed, but still pink inside. Distribute them evenly between the plates, and scatter the warmed croûtons and bits of bacon over them. Scatter the parsley and chives over each plateful, and serve with the mustardy French dressing handed separately in a jug with a spoon to stir up the contents.

Cucumber and Dill Soup

Cucumber has such an elegant, cool, distinctive summery taste, and this makes a perfect first course for a summer evening. It is convenient, too, in that it can be made entirely in the morning. I like to leave the skin on the cucumber before liquidizing it, because I love the tiny flecks of dark green. We need never fear a bitter cucumber these days, all possible bitterness has been bred out of commercially grown cucumbers. By scooping out the seeds, all potential indigestibility is removed, and any wateriness as well.

SERVES 6

2 cucumbers	*2 large handfuls of dill*
1 oz/28 g butter + 1 tbsp	*weed, chopped – remove*
sunflower oil	*any stalks*
1 onion, skinned and finely	*1 pt/570 ml creamy fromage*
chopped	*frais*
1 pt/570 ml chicken stock	*Salt and freshly ground*
	black pepper to your taste

Cut each cucumber in chunks, then each chunk in half lengthways, and scoop away the seeds.

Melt the butter and heat the oil in a saucepan and add the chopped onion. Cook for 2 or 3 minutes, then pour in the stock. Simmer gently for 10 minutes. Cool, then liquidize this with the chunks of cucumber, the dill weed and the fromage frais. Taste, and add salt and pepper to your liking.

Keep in a covered bowl in the fridge till you are ready to ladle it into soup plates or bowls. It looks so pretty I think it needs no garnishing.

Herb and Mushroom Crêpes

These make a substantial first course, so they need a simple main course to follow. They are delicious, and so useful in that they can be made in the morning, ready to reheat before supper – all you need to do is to pop the dish into a moderately hot oven. Putting chopped herbs into the pancake batter make the crêpes taste even better. These days we can buy fresh herbs so easily, all year round, and it adds a whole new dimension to our cooking.

SERVES 6

For the crêpes:
*2 large eggs broken into a
  food processor or
  liquidizer with 4 oz/112 g
  plain flour*
*½ pt/285 ml milk + 2 tbsp
  cold water*
*Salt and freshly ground
  black pepper*
*2 tbsp chopped parsley
  and snipped chives,
  mixed*
Butter for frying

For the mushroom filling:
*3 oz/84 g butter + 2 tbsp
  sunflower oil*
*1 lb/450 g mushrooms,
  wiped and chopped quite
  small*
*1 clove of garlic, skinned
  and finely chopped*
2 oz/56 g flour
1 pt/570 ml milk
*Salt and freshly ground
  black pepper*
A grating of nutmeg
*Finely chopped parsley and
  freshly grated Parmesan
  cheese, mixed*

Whiz the eggs and flour, adding the milk and water gradually. Add the salt, pepper, parsley and chives, then pour this batter into a jug and leave to stand for half an hour. Make up the crêpes by melting a tiny bit of butter in your crêpe pan and swirling it round. When it is foaming hot, pour in a small amount of batter, swirling it, too, around so that you get an even, very thin covering of batter over the base of the crêpe pan. Cook for a few seconds, then turn the crêpe over – I find the easiest way to do this is to slip my thumbs under the crêpe and flip it over. Cook for a further few seconds on the other side, then slip the cooked crêpe on to a tray to cool. Once cooled, stack the crêpes on a plate with a strip of greaseproof paper between each. Cover the finished stack of crêpes with clingfilm.

Make the filling by melting the butter and heating the oil together in a saucepan and cooking the chopped mushrooms in this, with the chopped garlic. When the mushrooms are very well cooked, stir in the flour. Cook for a minute, then gradually stir in the milk, stirring continuously till the sauce boils. Season with salt and pepper, and a grating of nutmeg. Press wet greaseproof paper on to the top of the sauce and leave to cool – this prevents a skin forming.

When cold, put a spoonful of the mushroom mixture in the middle of each crêpe – I allow two per person with possibly a few over. Roll the crêpe into a fat parcel by folding one side over, then the next, and so on till you have fat square. Put the stuffed crêpes on a buttered heatproof dish.

When the crêpes are completed, scatter them with the parsley and Parmesan mixture, cover and keep in a cool place till you are ready to reheat them for supper. Do this by putting the dish into a moderate oven, 350°F/180°C/Gas Mark 4, for about 20 minutes.

Asparagus Salad

I do love to make the most of things like asparagus when they are in season, but I only like to buy them when they are in their natural season to this country. I know that asparagus can be bought all year round imported from all over the world, but I just don't think it tastes the same. Another thing I personally loathe is the vogue for undercooking food, asparagus included. It has a different taste from when asparagus is cooked through, and not a nice taste at all in my opinion. On the other hand, it is a perfect waste to overcook asparagus, and I think the best way to cook it is to steam it. Stick a fork into the thickest spear and it should feel just tender.

Asparagus goes so well with egg, and also with prawns, but if you can't get or don't like prawns, just leave them out of this salad and increase the amount of asparagus.

SERVES 6

---

1 lb/450 g asparagus spears	*6 hardboiled eggs, shelled and chopped*
Assorted salad greenery	*Mayonnaise (I think*
12 oz/340 g shelled prawns	*mayonnaise is nicer with*
– if they are the big	*this salad than French*
juicy prawns, chop	*dressing)*
them	

Steam the asparagus till just tender. Refresh under cold water, then pat dry with kitchen paper.

Arrange the salad greenery on six plates. Put a small heap of asparagus in the middle, and scatter with the prawns, chopped or not, and the chopped hardboiled eggs. Hand the mayonnaise in a separate bowl.

Serve with warm granary bread or rolls.

More than Just the Family

Oysters on Mushroo.ns with Hollandaise Sauce

Stir-Fried Oysters with Ginger and Spring Onions

Venison Fillet with Port and Redcurrant Jelly

Chicken Liver and Mushroom Millefeuille

Baked Creamy Crab

Barbecued Oysters with Savoury Rice

Fillet of Sea Bass with Almonds

Venison Steaks with Red Wine and Vegetable Sauce

Monkfish in Gruyère Cheese Soufflé with Tomato Sauce

Braised Beef in Beaujolais

Hot Ham Mousse

Chicken and Tarragon Soufflé with Lemon Cream Sauce

Seafood Puff Pastry Turnover

Plaice (or Sole) on Spinach in Cheese Soufflé

Chicken and Avocado Salad

Asparagus Puff Pastry Parcels with Sauce Bercy

Baked Salmon with Sesame Vegetables

MORE THAN JUST THE FAMILY

The contents of this chapter are intended for those evenings when supper needs to be just that little bit more special than the usual everyday demands – the sort of occasion when you have someone other than the family as well, and although there is no need for a full-blown dinner party, you want to provide a supper which will extend the sociability of the meal, prolong the time spent sitting round the table (always my favourite time, whatever meal).

There is no need to be out to impress, just to make the extra person or people feel that you have gone to a small amount of trouble on their behalf to make supper a bit more than everyday. So you may want to add a first course – there is no need for a pud, too, unless you really want to push the boat out, but a bowl of fresh fruit and two or three cheeses and, as far as I'm concerned, some good chocolate to eat with coffee, makes a perfect supper for such an occasion. The recipes can in several cases be made ahead or, in some cases, prepared ahead, at your convenience.

Oysters on Mushrooms with Hollandaise Sauce

As cultivated shellfish becomes so much more readily available to us, I love to make the most of it. For most people shellfish is a very real treat, and therefore perfect for a main course for more than just the family. For the unfortunate few who are allergic to shellfish, or to one species of shellfish (because I know people who can't eat prawns, or crab, but who can eat other types of shellfish), it is only fair to warn anyone for whom you haven't cooked very frequently if you intend to give them shellfish; they will instantly tell you if they can or can't eat it. Oysters used to be such a staple diet for the British, and I sincerely hope that they will become so again, as the cultivated oysters increase in quantity year by year. I loathe raw oysters, but love them cooked. In this recipe they are briefly cooked beneath the hollandaise sauce under a hot grill.

This is a rich dish, and I think it is best accompanied by warm bread or rolls, and a good salad.

SERVES 6

Allow 5–6 oysters per person; they are, like all shellfish, filling

2 oz/56 g butter + 1 tbsp sunflower oil

1 small onion, red if possible, skinned and finely chopped

1 lb/450 g mushrooms, wiped, stalks trimmed level with the caps, and finely chopped

Salt and freshly ground black pepper

For the hollandaise sauce:

10 oz/285 g butter

5 large egg yolks

4 tbsp lemon juice, very gently simmered in a pan with 1 slice of onion and a few crushed parsley stalks (the crushing releases their flavour)

Salt and freshly ground black pepper

Shell the oysters. Have six individual ovenproof dishes warmed.

Melt the butter and heat the oil in a frying pan and cook the finely chopped onion for a minute or two, stirring so that it cooks evenly. Then turn up the heat and add the chopped mushrooms and, stirring slowly but continuously, cook the mushrooms well. Season with salt and pepper, and put some of this mushroom mixture in the base of each serving dish, spreading it evenly. Put the oysters, evenly spaced, on the mushroom mixture.

Make the hollandaise sauce by melting the butter in a saucepan, and heating it well. Put the yolks into a food processor and whiz, then, still whizzing, gradually add the very hot butter in a steady stream. When it is all added and you have a smooth sauce, whiz in the strained lemon juice. Taste, add salt and pepper to your liking, then pour this sauce over the oysters and mushrooms.

Heat a grill till very hot and pop the dishes on a baking tray under the grill for about 20–30 seconds. Serve as soon as you possibly can.

Stir-Fried Oysters
with Ginger and Spring Onions

This takes literally minutes to cook. You can shell the oysters and keep them in a covered bowl in the fridge till you are ready to cook. And you can peel and chop the ginger, and trim and slice the spring onions and keep them, too, in a covered bowl in the fridge, so all you need do just before eating is to cook them.

This is good with boiled Basmati rice, and a crunchy salad of sliced sugar snap peas, crisply cooked bacon and watercress. One of the good things about cooking with spring onions, quite apart from their flavour, is that their green colour intensifies in cooking.

SERVES 6

Depending on their size, allow 5–6 oysters per person (for a main course; 3 for a first course)	*18–20 good spring onions – not those weedy grass-thin ones*
About 2 in/5 cm fresh ginger	*3 tbsp sunflower oil*
	½ pt/285 ml single cream
	Salt and freshly ground black pepper

Shell the oysters. Pare the skin from the ginger and cut it into fine slivers. Trim the spring onions and slice them diagonally about ¼ in/0.5 cm thick.

Heat the oil in a wide shallow pan – a sauté or frying pan – and cook the ginger and spring onions, stirring continuously, for about 3 minutes. Then add the oysters and cook for a few seconds before pouring in the cream. Let the cream bubble for about a minute, season with salt and pepper, and tip into a warmed serving dish. Serve as soon as possible.

Venison Fillet with Port and Redcurrant Jelly

This is simple food, but excellent ingredients. How long you cook the meat depends on how rare you like to eat the venison. I like it just red in the very centre, but I loathe meat so underdone that it is almost bleeding on the plates.

This is nicest, I think, served with parboiled potatoes in their skins, chopped and sautéed till crisp, with paprika, and with a purée of root vegetables, such as Jerusalem artichokes or celeriac or parsnips. The best!

SERVES 6

2 oz/56 g butter + 2 tbsp sunflower oil	2 tsp redcurrant jelly – homemade if possible because it is less sweet than commercial
About 2 lb/900 g venison fillet, trimmed and left whole	Salt and freshly ground black pepper
½ pt/285 ml port	
½ pt/285 ml good stock	

In a wide sauté pan, heat the oil and melt the butter. Brown the fillet, turning it over and over so that it cooks evenly. Cook it like this for 10 minutes, then pour in the port and stock and stir in the jelly. Stir till the jelly melts – if it is homemade it will melt much more quickly than bought – and let the liquid bubble away around the meat till it reduces by about a third.

Lift the meat on to a board, and season the sauce in the pan with salt and pepper. Carve the meat into a warmed serving dish and pour the juices, the small amount of sauce, over the sliced meat.

Chicken Liver
and Mushroom Millefeuille

I find it such a help now that we can buy ready rolled out puff pastry. I can now make even-sized millefeuille! I loathe rolling out any type of pastry, I don't have the required touch, but now I find whole avenues of inspiring possibilities opened out for me. This is one. The chicken liver mixture, which is rich, is spread over the pastry, topped with the other bit, then baked, and the densely mushroomy sauce, spiked with Madeira, is served spooned beside each millefeuille.

These are filling, and I allow one per person. I like a green vegetable best with them, such as courgettes or sugar snap peas.

SERVES 6

---

1 lb/450 g rolled out puff pastry
2 oz/56 g butter
1 onion, skinned and finely chopped
1 clove of garlic, skinned and chopped
1½ lb/675 g chicken livers, picked over and chopped (the big bits)
Salt and freshly ground black pepper
A pinch of thyme
2 eggs, beaten

For the sauce:
2 oz/56 g butter + 2 tbsp sunflower oil
1 lb/450 g mushrooms, wiped, stalks cut level with the caps, and chopped
2 oz/56 g flour
½ pt/285 ml milk
½ pt/285 ml single cream
¼ pt/140 ml Madeira
Salt and freshly ground black pepper
A grating of nutmeg

Cut the pastry into twelve even-sized strips, each about 2 inches/5 cm wide.

Melt the butter in a saucepan and cook the onion and garlic in it till the onion is soft and transparent and just beginning to turn golden brown. Then raise the heat a bit and add the chopped chicken livers. Cook them briefly, till they seize up, season with salt and pepper, and with the thyme, and then take the pan off the heat and cool for 10 minutes. Then put the contents of the pan into a food processor and whiz till smooth.

Spread this mixture over six of the pieces of puff pastry. Put another piece of pastry on top of each, and brush them all over with the beaten egg. Put into the fridge

Make the mushroom sauce by melting the butter and heating the oil in a saucepan till very hot. Cook the chopped mushrooms over a fierce heat, stirring all the time, till they are almost crisp – this improves their flavour greatly. Then lower the heat, stir in the flour, cook for a minute, then gradually add the milk and cream, stirring continuously till the sauce boils. Stir in the Madeira, take the pan off the heat and season with the salt, pepper and nutmeg.

Bake the millefeuille in a hot oven, 400°F/200°C/Gas Mark 6, till they are well puffed up and golden, about 15–20 minutes. Serve as soon as possible, with the hot sauce. You can prepare the millefeuille in the morning if it is more convenient for you, all ready to bake that evening.

Baked Creamy Crab

Crab is rich, and crab is delicious! It is also very filling – I think all shellfish is. I usually prefer to eat crab cold, with mayonnaise and bread and butter, and a good salad. But there are occasions when we have certain people staying with us who I know prefer crab served hot in a cheesy sauce – and Godfrey far prefers crab and all shellfish in hot dishes rather than cold.

This needs boiled Basmati rice to accompany it, and a crunchy green vegetable, ideally sugar snap peas. If you precede this with a first course, choose something simple and un-rich, like a salad.

SERVES 6

3 oz/84 g butter	*¼ pt/140 ml dry sherry*
3 oz/84 g flour	*1½ lb/675 g crabmeat,*
1 tsp English mustard powder	*mixed brown and white*
1¼ pts/710 ml milk	*3 tbsp fresh breadcrumbs,*
Salt and pepper	*whizzed in a processor*
A grating of nutmeg	*with a handful of parsley*
A dash of Tabasco sauce	*– for scattering over the*
3 oz/84 g Cheddar cheese,	*surface*
grated	

Melt the butter in a saucepan and stir in the flour and the mustard powder. Cook for a minute before gradually pouring in the milk, stirring continuously till the sauce boils. Take the pan off the heat and stir in the seasonings and grated cheese, and the sherry. Leave the sauce to cool, then stir together the sauce and the crab. Pour this into an ovenproof dish, and scatter the parsley breadcrumbs over the surface.

Bake in a moderate oven, 350°F/180°C/Gas Mark 4, for 20–25 minutes – till the sauce bubbles. Heat a grill, and pop the dish from the oven under the grill, to toast the crumbs on top to a golden brown. Serve as soon as possible.

Barbecued Oysters with Savoury Rice

Shellfish and pieces of fish barbecue beautifully provided they are first wrapped in bacon. The taste of bacon enhances that of all fish and shellfish, and when barbecuing, the bacon serves a double purpose, not only as a taste-enhancer, but also as a shield against the shellfish getting too dry during cooking. There is another way to barbecue oysters (and mussels, too, for that matter) and that is to put them on the barbecue in their shells. As they cook, the shells will open. The way of cooking rice is foolproof and gives a slightly different way of serving rice to go with these oysters.

If you like, and I do, a well-flavoured mayonnaise can accompany the barbecued oysters and rice, needing only a good herb-filled green salad as the other accompaniment.

First make a most useful barbecue cooking implement. If you can, get hold of an Aga toasting contraption. If you can't, make a square or oblong double frame about 8″ × 12″, hinged at one end (like a scallop shell), and cover the frame with a double thickness of small-meshed chicken wire.

SERVES 6

Allow 5–6 oysters per person	For the rice:
	3 tblsp olive oil
15 rashers of streaky bacon, each rasher stretched on a board with a knife – it will lengthen by half as much again; cut each rasher in half, once lengthened	*1 onion, skinned and finely chopped*
	1 clove of garlic, skinned and finely chopped
	12 oz/340 g Basmati rice
	2 pts/1.1 L chicken stock
	2 tbsp finely chopped parsley

Wrap each oyster in a half-rasher of bacon and arrange these on one side of the wire-covered frame.

Make the rice by heating the oil in a saucepan and adding the finely chopped onion. Cook for 2–3 minutes, stirring, then add the chopped garlic and the rice. Cook for a couple of minutes, stirring, so that each grain of rice is coated in oil. Then pour in enough stock to come an inch/2.5 cm above the level of the rice. As you first pour the stock into the pan there will be a whoosh of steam – let this subside, so that you can see the level of stock over the rice. Put a folded teatowel over the pan and put a lid on top – don't stir once the stock has been added. Put the pan on a low temperature hotplate and leave for 5 minutes, then take the pan off the heat and leave for 15 minutes. The rice in the saucepan will have absorbed all the stock. Just before turning the rice into a serving dish, fork the chopped parsley through it.

Five minutes before you want to eat, when the barbecue coals are white hot and there are no red flames, put the wire contraption holding the oysters on the grill. Cook for about 2 minutes, then turn the toaster over and cook for a further couple of minutes on the other side. Serve.

Fillet of Sea Bass with Almonds

I love the way people are eating so much more fish these days. Along with our growing appreciation of fish has come a desire to experiment with the different types of fish we cook. It is several years since we first cooked sea bass, a firm-fleshed fish which is versatile because of its robustness. In this recipe it is baked on a bed of parsley, then served with a creamy mushroom and almond sauce. It's quick to cook, but makes a delicious and elegant main course for a supper when you are more than just the family.

SERVES 6

2–3 good handfuls of
  parsley
2¹/₂–3 lb/1.125–1.35 kg
  filleted sea bass
Butter
For the sauce:
2 oz/56 g butter and 1 tbsp
  sunflower oil
1 red onion, skinned and
  finely chopped

¹/₂ lb/225 g mushrooms,
  wiped, stalks cut level
  with each cap, and
  chopped
3 oz/84 g flaked almonds,
  toasted till pale golden
¹/₂ pt/285 ml single cream
Salt and freshly ground
  black pepper

Butter a pyrex or similarly ovenproof dish well. Put the parsley over the base of the dish, and lay the fillets of sea bass on the parsley. Dot with bits of butter and cover the dish with foil, tightly. You can prepare the fish to this stage in the morning, all ready to pop the dish into the oven – but if you can, take the dish out of the fridge an hour before you cook it, otherwise the fish will take longer to cook, straight from fridge to oven. Bake in a moderate oven, 350°F/180°C/Gas Mark 4, for 15–20 minutes – till the fish is cooked when you gently stick a fork in the thickest bit.

To make the sauce, melt the butter and heat the oil together in a saucepan. Add the finely chopped onion and cook for several minutes, stirring, till the onion is soft, transparent-looking and beginning to turn golden. Add the mushrooms, and cook till they are well done. Add the almonds, the cream, a pinch of salt and lots of black pepper. Simmer the sauce for a minute or two, then pour it into a warmed serving bowl. Alternatively, serve the fish on to warmed plates with the sauce spooned over it.

Venison Steaks
with Red Wine and Vegetable Sauce

For this recipe you need to cut thick slices of a fillet of venison. They are cooked in a red wine sauce with tiny onions and julienne strips of carrot and parship. The whole dish can be made in advance and reheated to serve.

I think it is nicest served with creamily mashed potatoes with plenty of parsley and chives beaten into them, and with either a green salad or a green vegetable, such as steamed spring greens or stir-fried cabbage, to accompany it.

SERVES 6

2½ lb/1.125 kg venison
fillet, cut into thick
slices

2 tbsp flour mixed well
with ½ tsp salt and
plenty of ground black
pepper

3–4 tbsp sunflower oil

1 lb/450 g tiny onions,
skinned by pouring
boiling water over them
in a bowl; leave them for
a minute, drain off the
water and snip off their
ends – the onions should
pop out of their skins
when squeezed

3 carrots and 3 parsnips,
each peeled and sliced
into neat matchsticks

1–2 cloves of garlic, each
skinned and finely
chopped

½ pt/285 ml red wine

¾ pt/420 ml water or stock

Coat the pieces of meat in the seasoned flour on each side. Heat the oil in a heavy casserole and quickly brown each slice of meat on each side, removing them, as they brown, to a warmed dish. Lower the heat a bit and add the onions, carrots, parsnips and garlic. Cook, stirring occasionally to prevent them sticking, for about 15 minutes – they will be almost cooked through. Stir in the wine and water (or stock), stirring till the sauce bubbles. Replace the meat in the sauce, pushing it down amongst the vegetables.

Cover with a lid, and cook the casserole in a moderate oven, 350°F/180°C/Gas Mark 4, for 25–30 minutes. Alternatively, if you prepare the casserole up to the stage where you replace the meat, you can cool it completely and store it in the fridge, ready to cook that evening. Remember to take it from the fridge into room temperature an hour before cooking it, or if you can't, give it an extra 20 minutes' cooking time.

Monkfish in Gruyère Cheese Soufflé with Tomato Sauce

Monkfish is such a robust fish. I love it for several reasons – chiefly for its taste and texture. In years past, monkfish used to be cut up and dipped in those vile orange breadcrumbs and served as scampi. There must have been (perhaps still are) countless numbers of people who were none the wiser. It gives you some idea of its texture. It is easy to prepare in that it has no bones, just a central cartilage running down the middle of the tail – the tail is the part of the monkfish that you eat. It is simplicity itself to slice the fillet of fish either side of this cartilage type of bone.

This is a cheesy soufflé spiked with mustard and a drop of balsamic vinegar to sharpen up the flavour. The tomato sauce can be made well in advance and reheated – its taste complements that of the fish and cheese soufflé, but it also looks attractive.

SERVES 6

2 lb/900 g monkfish tails –
  weighed when cut from
  their bone; cut the fish
  into chunks about 1–1½
  in/3–4 cm in size
3 oz/84 g butter
3 oz/84 g self-raising flour
2 tsp English mustard
  powder
1¼ pts/710 ml milk
Salt and ground black
  pepper
1 tsp balsamic vinegar
6 oz/170 g Gruyère cheese,
  grated
6 large eggs, separated

For the tomato sauce:
3 tbsp olive oil
2 onions, skinned and
  chopped
1 stick of celery, washed,
  trimmed and chopped
Two drained 15-oz/420-g
  tins of chopped tomatoes
Salt and pepper
A pinch of sugar
1 tsp pesto

Butter either one large ovenproof dish, or two smaller dishes of the same size – if you have two of differing sizes the smaller soufflé will be cooked before the larger.

Put the cut-up fish in the dish or dishes. Melt the butter in a large saucepan and stir in the flour and the mustard powder. Let this mixture cook for a minute, then, stirring all the time, pour in the milk gradually. Stir till the sauce bubbles, then take the pan off the heat and stir in the salt, pepper, balsamic vinegar and grated Gruyère, stirring till the cheese melts. Beat in the egg yolks, one by one. In a bowl whisk the egg whites with a pinch of salt – which gives a greater volume – till they are very stiff, then, with a large metal spoon, fold the whisked whites quickly and thoroughly through the cheese soufflé mixture, and pour this over the fish in the buttered dish or dishes.

Bake in a hot oven, 420°F/220°C/Gas Mark 7, for 35 minutes if you are using one dish. If two smaller ones, reduce the cooking time by 10 minutes. Serve immediately.

To make the sauce, heat the oil in a saucepan and cook the chopped onions till they are soft and beginning to turn golden brown at the edges, then add the celery and continue to cook for about 3–4 minutes more. Add the tomatoes, and stir in the salt, pepper, sugar and pesto. Simmer very gently for 15 minutes, then cool the sauce and liquidize it. Reheat it to serve.

Braised Beef in Beaujolais

The joy of this is that it can be made the day before and reheated to serve. As with virtually all casseroles, the flavour is very much better if it is made in advance. It is well worth taking the time to make the stew correctly, cutting no corners. The cooking of the onions at the beginning of any casserole, stew, or soup is, I think, all-important to the flavour of the end result. I loathe the taint of the taste of undercooked onions.

This is delicious served with either creamily mashed potatoes, or baked sliced potatoes, or sautéed potatoes.

3 lb/1.35 kg braising steak, trimmed and cut into 1½-in/4-cm chunks

2 tbsp flour with ½ tsp salt and plenty of ground black pepper mixed into it

2 oz/56 g butter + 2 tbsp sunflower oil

1 lb/450 g tiny onions, skinned by pouring boiling water over the onions in a bowl, leaving for 1 minute, then draining; snip the ends off the onions and they should pop neatly out of their skins with no trouble

6 rashers of back bacon, cut into small dice

½ lb/225 g mushrooms, wiped and sliced

2 cloves of garlic, skinned and finely chopped

1 bottle Beaujolais

Bouquet garni made by tying together a few parsley stalks, a sprig of thyme and a bayleaf

Coat the cut-up meat in the seasoned flour. Heat the oil and melt the butter together in a heavy casserole and brown the meat, a small amount at a time, removing it to a warm dish as it browns. If you try to brown the whole lot at one go it won't brown, it will lower the temperature in the casserole and the meat will stew in its juices. Once the meat is all browned, lower the temperature a bit and add the skinned onions and the diced bacon. Cook, stirring occasionally, till the onions are just beginning to turn colour, about 5–7 minutes. Add the sliced mushrooms and the chopped garlic, and cook for a few minutes before pouring in the wine. Stir till the sauce bubbles, then add the bouquet garni, replace the meat and cover the casserole with a lid.

Cook it in a moderate oven, 350°F/180°C/Gas Mark 4, for 1 hour. Cool, and store it in the fridge. To reheat, take it out of the fridge and into room temperature for an hour before putting it back into a moderate oven for a further hour's cooking.

Hot Ham Mousse

This is so easy to make. You can either serve it with the horseradish sauce, or if you prefer a rather less rich sauce you can substitute the tomato sauce on page 54 in the recipe for Monkfish in Gruyère Cheese Soufflé.

I like to serve leeks and tomatoes in vinaigrette to go with Hot Ham Mousse.

SERVES 6

1 lb/450 g cooked ham, trimmed of fat	*6 large eggs*
	2 tbsp dry sherry
³/₄ pt/420 ml single cream	Horseradish sauce:
A dash of Tabasco sauce	*4 tbsp dried horseradish*
Plenty of ground black pepper	*¹/₂ pt/285 ml crème fraîche*
	1 tsp sugar
A grating of nutmeg	*1 tbsp lemon juice*
	1 tsp wine vinegar

Butter a large soufflé dish, or two equal-sized smaller dishes. Put the ham into a food processor and whiz till fine, then, still whizzing, add the cream, Tabasco, pepper and nutmeg. Continue to whiz and add 2 whole eggs, then the yolks of the remaining 4 eggs, and the sherry. In a bowl, whisk the whites with a pinch of salt (to give a greater volume) till they are very stiff. With a large metal spoon fold the whites quickly and thoroughly into the ham mixture and pour this into the buttered dish, or dishes.

Bake in a roasting tin with water in it to a depth of 1 inch/2½ cm, in a moderate oven, 350°F/180°C/Gas Mark 4, for 55–60 minutes for the large dish or 45–50 minutes if using two smaller ones.

Mix all the ingredients for the horseradish sauce together and serve it in a bowl to hand round with the mousse.

Chicken and Tarragon Soufflé with Lemon Cream Sauce

To make the flavoured milk for the sauce which, along with the chicken, is the basis of this soufflé, may sound a bit of a fiddle, but it really doesn't take a minute and the end result is so worthwhile.

This is a delicately flavoured soufflé, enhanced by the lemon sauce. It needs a crunchy accompanying vegetable – I suggest sugar snap peas stir-fried with spring onions and a small amount of chopped fresh ginger, or a good mixed salad. Warm granary bread or rolls is the only other accompaniment needed.

SERVES 6

For the flavoured milk:
1 pt/570 ml milk
1 onion, skinned and cut in half
A small bunch of crushed parsley stalks
½ tsp salt – rock salt if possible, and 2 tsp peppercorns
For the chicken soufflé:
2 oz/56 g butter
2 oz/56 g flour
Strained flavoured milk
1 lb/450 g cooked chicken

5 tarragon leaves
5 large eggs, separated
For the lemon cream sauce:
2 oz/56 g butter
1 tsp flour
3 egg yolks
1 tsp mustard powder
½ pt/285 ml milk
Grated rind and juice of 1 well washed and dried lemon
1 tbsp finely chopped parsley and snipped chives, mixed

Put the milk in a saucepan with all the flavouring ingredients and bring it to scalding point. When a skin forms, take the pan off the heat and leave for 1 hour. Strain the milk into a jug.

Butter a large ovenproof dish or two smaller, even-sized dishes. Make a white sauce by melting the butter in a large saucepan and stirring in the flour. Let it cook for a minute then, stirring continuously, gradually add the milk. Stir till the sauce boils, then take the pan off the heat.

Put the chicken into a processor with the tarragon leaves and whiz till it is finely minced. Whiz in the egg yolks, one by one, and lastly the white sauce. Whisk the egg whites in a bowl with a pinch of salt till they are very stiff and, with a large metal spoon, fold them quickly and thoroughly into the chicken mixture. Pour this into the prepared dish or dishes.

Bake in a roasting tin with water to a depth of 1–2 inches/2½–5 cm in a moderate oven, 350°F/180°C/Gas Mark 4, for 45 minutes if one large dish is used or 35 minutes for two smaller dishes. Serve immediately.

To make the sauce, put the butter, flour, egg yolks, mustard powder, milk and lemon rind into an ovenproof bowl, place it over a saucepan of gently simmering water and let the butter melt, stirring with a flat wire whisk from time to time. The sauce will gradually thicken. It will take 20–25 minutes, depending on the depth of water the bowl is sitting in. When the sauce has thickened to the point where it is like thick cream, take the bowl off the heat, and just before serving stir in the lemon juice and mixed herbs.

Seafood Puff Pastry Turnover

You can vary the contents of your turnovers to suit availability of ingredients where you live, but these days it is getting easier and easier to buy shellfish, due to the increase in cultivated items like scallops, mussels and oysters, and it is really almost easier in some parts of Britain to buy these than any fish slightly out of the ordinary, such as hake or monkfish. As the fish cooks in the pastry it steams, really the best way to cook shellfish and fish.

With the turnovers there is no need for potatoes, nor any other form of starch, but a vegetable such as my current favourite, sugar snap peas (I never want to see another mangetout, they are so dreary in comparison with the sugar snaps), and a good herb-filled green salad would be ideal accompaniments.

SERVES 6

1¹/₂ lb/675 g ready rolled out puff pastry	*shelled, and each cut in half – weighed after shelling*
1¹/₂ lb/675 g trimmed monkfish, cut into 1-inch/ 2.5-cm bits	*2 oz/56 g butter, melted, then cooled just enough before it firms up*
6 scallops	*2 tbsp chopped parsley*
18 shelled mussels	*1 tbsp chopped dill weed*
¹/₂ lb/225 g large prawns, cooked for 30 seconds in boiling water then	*1 egg, beaten*

Cut six large circles from the pastry, each about 6 inches/15 cm in diameter. Cut each scallop in three bits. Mix together in a bowl all the fish and shellfish, the cooled butter, parsley and dill weed. Spoon this mixture on to one side of each circle. Fold the other over, and stick it down with a little beaten egg. Put each turnover on a baking tray – no need to butter or oil it first – and brush each one with the beaten egg.

Bake in an oven at 400°F/200°C/Gas Mark 6, for 20 minutes. If you like, serve with the Sauce Bercy given for Asparagus Puff Pastry Parcels on page 63.

Plaice (or Sole) on Spinach in Cheese Soufflé

This is really a version of eggs florentine using fish instead of eggs, and the whole cooked in a cheese soufflé rather than with just a cheese sauce poured over. I love plaice, and I always think it grossly unfair that dreary old lemon sole gets a far higher rating than the humbler plaice. Plaice has far more taste than lemon sole, and I can only think that it's because the name 'sole' has connotations in people's minds with the far more worthy and aristocratic Dover member of the sole family.

The spinach in this recipe can be prepared well in advance. So can the cheese soufflé mixture for that matter – it won't come to any harm provided it is kept closely covered with clingfilm.

Garlic bread or warmed granary bread or rolls go very well with this.

SERVES 6

---

3 lb/1.35 kg fresh spinach	*2 oz/56 g flour*
2 oz/56 g butter	*1 pt/570 ml milk*
Salt and ground black	*6 oz/170 g good Cheddar*
pepper	*cheese, grated*
A grating of nutmeg	*Salt and ground black*
1½ lb/675 g filleted, skinned	*pepper*
plaice	*A grating of nutmeg*
For the cheese soufflé:	*4 large eggs, separated*
2 oz/56 g butter	

I know this sounds like a lot of spinach, and when you see it you will have a fit and think 'Has she taken leave of her senses?', but anyone who has cooked spinach will know that it decreases horrifically. Steam the spinach till it wilts. Then put it into a food processor and whiz it, adding the butter, salt, pepper and nutmeg. Butter a wide ovenproof dish and spread the puréed spinach over the base of this dish. When the spinach has cooled, put the plaice in a thick layer on top of it.

Make the soufflé by melting the butter and stirring in the flour. Cook for a minute, then, stirring continuously, gradually add the milk. Stir till the sauce boils. Take the pan off the heat and stir in the grated cheese, stirring till it melts, and stir in the salt, pepper and nutmeg. Beat in the egg yolks, one by one. Lastly, whisk the whites till they are very stiff, adding a pinch of salt (which gives increased volume), and then, with a large metal spoon, fold the whites quickly and thoroughly through the cheese mixture. Pour this over the fish.

Either cover the dish with clingfilm ready to cook two or three hours later, or bake it straight away in a hot oven, 420°F/220°C/Gas Mark 7, for 25 minutes. Serve immediately.

Chicken and Avocado Salad

The excellence of this salad depends on the ingredients – the chicken must be moist, not dried either during its cooking or in its leftover state. The avocados must be tip-top quality. If that is the case, this salad is delicious, and not only delicious to eat, perfect supper food for an occasion when you are more than just the family, but also interesting to eat, with the other ingredients providing contrasting textures – the toasted flaked almonds, the crispness of the very finely sliced celery, and the fresh taste and slight crunch of the cucumber.

If you can't get crème fraîche, use double cream whipped with the juice of half a lemon. But as we can buy very good crème fraîche in the Co-op in Broadford here in Skye, I'm quite sure you can buy it anywhere in the British Isles.

SERVES 6

4 avocado pears

Juice of 1 lemon

1 lb/450 g white cooked chicken meat, cut into ½-in/1-cm dice

2 sticks of celery, each washed and trimmed and very finely sliced

½ cucumber, skin pared off with a potato peeler, the cucumber then cut in half lengthways and all the

centre seeds scooped away, the flesh cut into fine dice

2 oz/56 g flaked almonds, dry-fried in a pan over moderate heat till pale golden

6 tbsp crème fraîche

1 teaspoon paprika

Salt and ground black pepper to your taste

Chopped parsley – optional

With a sharp knife cut each avocado in half and flick out the stone. With the tip of the knife, score down each half of the skin to make three strips and peel these away. Cut the avocado into dice about the same size as the chicken, and carefully toss them in lemon juice, to help prevent discolouring.

In a bowl, carefully, so as not to break up the avocado dice and reduce them to mush, mix together all the ingredients. Then spoon into a decorative serving bowl. Sprinkle with parsley if you like.

Asparagus Puff Pastry Parcels with Sauce Bercy

This is delicious for carnivores as well as for vegetarians. Although we can buy asparagus all year round, I much prefer to wait till it comes into our natural season to Britain. I think it tastes better.

As with the Seafood Turnovers, I don't think these asparagus parcels need potatoes or rice with them, just something like a tomato and basil salad, and perhaps roast aubergines, garlic and peppers.

SERVES 6

2 lb/900 g asparagus	For the sauce Bercy:
2 oz/56 g butter	*2 red onions, each skinned,*
Salt and ground black pepper	*sliced and very finely chopped*
A grating of nutmeg	*½ pt/285 ml dry white wine*
1½ lb/675 g ready rolled out puff pastry	*8 oz/225 g butter, cut in bits about 1 oz/28 g each*
1 egg, beaten	*Salt and black pepper*

First, trim any really tough ends off the asparagus stalks. Cut the head off each stalk and set aside. Steam the stalks till barely tender, then put them in a food processor and whiz them with the 2 oz/56 g butter till they are a smooth purée. Season with salt and pepper and a grating of nutmeg. While your steamer is on, steam the heads of the asparagus for 1 minute, no more. Set on one side.

Cut six circles in the pastry. Spread half of each with the asparagus purée, and divide the asparagus heads evenly between them, laying them on top of the purée. Fold the other half of each circle over, and seal with beaten egg, pressing the edges down. Put the semi-circles on a baking tray – no need to butter or oil it. Brush the asparagus parcels with beaten egg.

Bake in an oven at 400°F/200°C/Gas Mark 6 for about 20 minutes, or till the parcels are puffed and golden.

Make the sauce by putting the very finely chopped onions into a saucepan with the wine and simmering gently till the wine has reduced almost completely. The onions will be almost pulpy. Beat in the bits of butter, one at a time, till it is all incorporated and you have a smooth, buttery sauce. Season with salt and pepper to your taste. Serve a spoonful beside each asparagus parcel.

Baked Salmon with Sesame Vegetables

For this I cook the salmon in the best way I know, as taught me by John Tovey.

SERVES 6

1½–2 lb/675–900 g fresh salmon, filleted, skinned and cut into 6 equal-sized pieces
6 oz/170 g butter
1 tbsp sesame oil
2 in/5 cm fresh root ginger, pared of its skin and very finely chopped
1 clove garlic, skinned and very finely chopped

3 leeks, trimmed and sliced into very fine strips
2 carrots, peeled and sliced as finely as possible
6 oz/170 g sugar snap peas, sliced diagonally (because it looks nicer)
Salt and freshly ground black pepper

Put the pieces of salmon on a baking tray (unbuttered) and put a 1-oz/28-g piece of butter on top of each. Bake in a hot oven, 400°F/200°C/Gas Mark 6, for 5 minutes.

Heat the oil in a non-stick frying or sauté pan and, over high heat, add the ginger, garlic, leeks and carrots to the pan. Stir-fry for about 4–5 minutes, then add the sliced sugar snap peas. Cook, stirring, for a further minute or two, season to your taste, and serve a spoonful of the sesame vegetables beside each piece of salmon, for a delicious but very healthy main course.

Sunday Suppers

Black Olive, Sun-Dried Tomato and Garlic Bread

Cheese, Mustard and Garlic Granary Bread

Minestrone

Onion Soup with Cheese Croûtons

Fish and Vegetable Chowder

Julienne of Root Vegetables Soup

Potato and Leek Soup

Scrambled Eggs with Smoked Haddock and Grilled Tomatoes

Black Pudding with Baked Apples

Mushroom Meringue

Eggs Benedict

Baked Eggs on Chopped Ham, Mushrooms and Garlic

Chive and Tomato Omelette with Cottage Cheese

Welsh Rarebit

Herring Roes with Sesame Toast and Grilled Bacon

Rice in Chicken Stock with Mushrooms and Garlic

Camembert and Bacon Omelette

SUNDAY SUPPERS

Supper on a Sunday differs from that on any other night of the week in that, for most families, it follows a large lunch. I read recently an article by Nicholas Coleridge saying that very few of his friends, when canvassed, would admit to eating a lunch on Sunday which involved roast meat, as in the traditional Sunday lunch in Britain. But he then went on to give such a farcical estimate of the price of a rib of beef for roasting that I thought either his friends must have been having him on or he must have misunderstood them. Because whether you have roast meat, chicken or game, or a steak and kidney pie or pudding, or whatever, the pattern of eating, certainly in the winter months, certainly for families, involves the reversal of that on the other six days of the week – a larger lunch is eaten, and a smaller and as effort-free as possible supper.

Now our 'children' (this really is an inaccurate description – by the time this book is published Alexandra, our eldest, will be married and, hopefully, qualified as a nurse!) are older, they very often get their own supper, and Sunday is the one night of the week when there is a sort of à la carte supper, but each providing for themselves, although we always sit down to our various suppers together. Given the choice, I opt for baked halved tomatoes on toasted granary bread spread with butter and marmite. The choices for the rest of our family vary, but often incorporate what is more usually thought of as breakfast food – scrambled eggs, bacon, sausages, that sort of thing.

But, as is often the case, when we have friends staying with us (as opposed to our hotel guests) it is much easier to have one thing for supper for all. And that is what the contents of this chapter contain, suggestions for supper on a Sunday which are all delicious, and which in many cases can be made or prepared in advance. There are a couple of bread recipes, which dress up a good soup, and there are breakfast type of things – like the Scrambled Eggs with Smoked Haddock, and the black pudding with baked apples. Many of the recipes can be prepared and made by keen and helpful children – who should all be encouraged enthusiastically, in my opinion!

Black Olive, Sun-Dried Tomato and Garlic Bread

I made this recipe first in the early summer of 1992, making it up as I went along. Initially I tried baking it in oiled loaf tins, as I do the bread we make each day here, using granary flour. But I didn't like the texture that resulted from that.

Then I discovered that in my enthusiasm I was using too much olive oil. This revelation came via the Chubb inspector of our fire extinguishers, who arrived one day as I was happily kneading away, and gazed long and thoughtfully at my bread-making (sadly not at me!). Then, unable to contain himself any longer, he rushed to the sink and washed his hands, and said 'Here, let me have a go.' He took over my kneading with the sure touch of an expert and told me that he had been a master baker till he was made redundant and got a job with Chubb. I learnt so much from him in twenty minutes! Amongst the tips was that the amount of olive oil I was using was too much for the flour, and my olive and garlic, etc., bread has been better ever since!

This is delicious whatever the time of year, and freezes as well as any other type of loaf, which is excellently. But beware of ever trying to fast-thaw any baked goods in a microwave – I think it draws the moisture out of all baked items, bread included, and the bread feels day-old. Two or three hours at room temperature thaws most loaves.

THIS MAKES 1 LOAF

½ pt/285 ml hand-hot water with 1 tsp sugar stirred in, and 1 tbsp of dried yeast (I use Allinson's) stirred in well; leave this mixture in a warm place till a head of froth develops equal in size to the amount of liquid underneath

1 lb/450 g strong plain white flour sieved with 1 tsp salt

About 12 good, juicy black olives – preferably ones which have been kept in oil, not beastly brine – stoned and chopped

2 large cloves of garlic,

skinned and finely	*tomatoes preserved in oil,*
chopped	*chopped*
About half a jar of sun-dried	*1 tbsp olive oil*

When the yeast has frothed up, mix it into the flour, along with the olives, garlic, sun-dried tomatoes and oil. Mix all together well, then knead, on a floured surface, till the dough feels elastic and smooth. Shape the dough into a fat sausage, put this on an oiled baking tray and leave, uncovered, till the dough has doubled in size – this will only take 10–15 minutes if the kitchen is warm.

Bake in a very hot oven, 420°F/220°C/Gas Mark 7 for 10–15 minutes. After 10 minutes, turn the loaf over and tap its base, which should sound hollow. If it doesn't, put the loaf back for a further few minutes' cooking. Cool on a wire rack but in a warm place – cooling bread (or cake, for that matter) in a cold place, or in a draught, toughens the dough.

Cheese, Mustard and Garlic Granary Bread

This amount makes three loaves – you can eat one and freeze the other two. This bread is quite delicious eaten as bread, but it is also delicious toasted – with scrambled eggs, or as an accompnaiment to soup of any kind. Don't be put off by the amount of garlic in the ingredients – it seems to me that garlic gets lost in the bread, and you really do need as much as I advocate to make the presence of the garlic felt. The mustard just enhances the cheese.

MAKES 3 LOAVES

---

¹/₂pt/285ml hand-hot water with 2 tsp sugar stirred in and 1¹/₂ oz/42g dried yeast (I use Allinson's) stirred in well; leave this yeast and water mixture in a warm place till a head of froth develops equal in size to the water underneath – you need a plastic or a pyrex bowl to enable you to see

1¹/₄pts/710 ml hot water with 1 tbsp salt and 2 tbsp demerara sugar stirred into it

3 lb/1.35 kg granary flour (if you prefer, you can substitute ordinary wholemeal flour)

3 large cloves of garlic, skinned and finely chopped

2 tsp English mustard powder

6 oz/170 g strong Cheddar cheese, grated

When the yeast has frothed up, mix it and the salt-and-sugar water into the flour, adding the garlic, mustard powder and grated cheese. Mix all well together, then turn the dough on to a floured work surface and knead – I count to 200, to give you some idea of how long you need to knead (sorry!). The dough will be smooth and elastic. Divide the dough into three equal pieces, and knead each one, then put each into an oiled loaf tin (I use 2-lb/900g loaf tins, three of them). Leave the tins in a warm place but not on direct heat, covering them with a cloth.

Bake the bread in a hot oven 420°F–220°C/Gas Mark 7, for 15–20 minutes – the loaves should sound hollow when tapped on their bases. Cool them on a wire cooling rack, in a warm place – cooling them in a cold place or in a draught will toughen the dough. Wrap and freeze any loaves you don't intend to eat that same day, once they have cooled.

Minestrone

I would find it hard to pick one favourite soup out of my repertoire, but this one comes, if not top, then very near to the top of my list. It is an invaluable soup, being virtually a meal in itself. It freezes beautifully, and although it is in this chapter for Sunday night suppers, it is as useful and delicious at any lunch or light supper.

I serve a bowl of freshly grated Parmesan cheese with the Minestrone.

SERVES 6

3 tbsp olive oil

2 medium onions, each skinned and finely chopped

6 rashers of back bacon, most fat trimmed off, and meat finely diced

3 medium potatoes, peeled and chopped in neat, small dice

½ lb/225 g Brussels sprouts, outer leaves trimmed away, and each sprout chopped in 3 or 4 bits

2 carrots, peeled and chopped into small dice

3 sticks of celery, trimmed and finely sliced

A 15-oz/420-g tin of chopped tomatoes

2 pts/1.1 L chicken or beef stock

¼ pt/140 ml red wine

1 tsp pesto sauce

A 15-oz/420-g tin of baked beans

3 oz/84 g very tiny pasta – these are usually in star shapes, but minuscule

Salt and lots of freshly ground black pepper

A pinch of sugar

Heat the olive oil and add the chopped onions and diced bacon to the oil in a large saucepan. Cook, stirring occasionally, for about 5 minutes, then add the diced potatoes, Brussels sprouts, carrots and celery, and continue to cook, stirring from time to time, for several more minutes. Then pour in the chopped tomatoes, stock, wine and pesto, and let this mixture simmer very gently, with the pan half-covered with its lid.

Cook for 25–30 minutes. Before serving, stir in the baked beans and pasta, season with salt, pepper and the sugar, and simmer for a further 10 minutes.

Serve with Parmesan cheese.

Onion Soup with Cheese Croûtons

Not only is this delicious to eat, but eating plenty of onions and garlic is very good for you. This is a simple soup to prepare, but so good to eat – perfect Sunday night supper food. If you would rather serve the Cheese, Mustard and Garlic Granary bread with the soup, don't bother to make the Cheese Croûtons – both would be altogether too stodgy, and possibly have you writhing with indigestion!

SERVES 6

---

1 oz/28 g butter + 3 tbsp sunflower oil	*Salt and freshly ground black pepper to taste*
8 medium onions	For the cheese croûtons:
2 pts/1.1 L beef stock (you can use consommé if it's more convenient)	*6 slices of bread, crusts cut off*
3 cloves of garlic, skinned and very finely chopped	*Soft butter*
¼ pt/140 ml red wine	*8 oz/225 g good Cheddar or, better still, Lancashire cheese, grated*

To make the soup, melt the butter and heat the oil in a large saucepan. Skin the onions, and slice them very thinly. You can do this in a food processor with a slicing attachment, to help prevent painful weeping – otherwise slice near an open window, as this, too, helps. (Wearing contact lenses is a great boon, it also helps!)

Cook the thinly sliced onions in the hot oil and butter, stirring from time to time, till the onions are soft and turning golden. This takes time, and mustn't be hurried – the flavour of the soup is so very much better if you let the onions cook like this, even though it will take about 15 minutes. Then pour in the stock, add the finely chopped garlic (which would lose most of its taste if it was cooked from the start with the onions) and the red wine, and season with salt and pepper.

Let the soup simmer very gently, with the saucepan half-covered with its lid, for 20 minutes. Then either cool and store in the fridge till needed, or serve immediately, whichever is convenient.

To make the cheese croûtons, toast the bread slices on each side. Butter each very lightly – this is easy if the butter is soft. Press grated cheese over the surface of each piece of toast, and grill till the cheese has melted and is bubbling. Cut each slice of toasted cheese into small cubes, and scatter these over each plateful of soup.

Fish and Vegetable Chowder

This is a most sustaining soup, full of the lovely flavours of fish, shellfish, vegetables and saffron. It is much the best made then eaten straight away – if you make it in advance, I advise you not to add the tomato, fish or shellfish till you are going to reheat the soup. It is quite filling. The fish will cook in the soup if simmered gently for 5 minutes before serving.

SERVES 6

3 tbsp olive oil	*A good pinch of saffron*
1 onion, skinned and finely chopped	*strands (rather than powder)*
2 sticks of celery, trimmed and very finely sliced	*1½ lb/675 g mixed white fish, bones and skin removed, and flesh cut into 1-in/2.5-cm chunks*
1 blade of fennel, trimmed and chopped very small	

*1 carrot, peeled and sliced
into fine matchsticks*
*2 potatoes, peeled and
chopped into small dice*
1½ pts/850 ml fish stock
*Salt and freshly ground
black pepper*

*½ lb/225 g shellfish, e.g.
cooked mussels,
prawns, squid sliced in
circles*
*2 tomatoes, skinned, de-
seeded and sliced into
thin strips*
*1 tbsp finely chopped
parsley*

Heat the oil in a large saucepan and add the prepared vegetables *except* the strips of tomato. Cook the vegetables over a moderate heat, stirring occasionally to prevent them sticking to the bottom of the pan, for about 10 minutes. Pour in the fish stock, and simmer for 10 minutes. Taste, season with salt and pepper and stir in the saffron. Before serving, reheat the soup, add the fish, the shellfish and the tomato strips, and simmer the soup very gently for 5 minutes. Just before serving, stir the chopped parsley through the soup.

If you like, serve with toasted pieces of French bread floating on the surface, and a bowl of garlic mayonnaise well spiked with Tabasco sauce to spoon into the soup on top of the bread.

Julienne of Root Vegetables Soup

In the autumn, winter and early spring months I love to make the most of the wide variety of root vegetables available both in the garden and on the shelves of shops and supermarkets. This soup uses as wide a range as you can get, all very finely sliced into matchsticks – which takes no time at all if you have a mandolin. The basis of this soup is a good chicken stock – or, if you are cooking for non-meat eaters, a vegetable stock. The soup can be made two or three days in advance and kept in a covered container in the fridge, or it can be frozen if you are trying to get well ahead with your cooking. Allow it to thaw overnight in the fridge.

This is good served with the Cheese, Mustard and Garlic Granary Bread.

3 tbsp sunflower oil

2 onions, skinned and finely sliced

1 carrot and 1 parsnip, peeled and sliced into fine matchsticks

2 leeks, trimmed, washed and sliced into thin strips

4 sticks of celery, washed, trimmed and sliced into thin strips

3 beetroot (raw), peeled and sliced into thin matchsticks

½ lb/225 g Jerusalem artichokes (if you can get them – if not, increase the carrots and parsnips), peeled and thinly sliced

½ head of celeriac, peeled and sliced into fine matchsticks

1–2 cloves of garlic, skinned and finely chopped

2 pts/1.1 L good chicken or vegetable stock

Salt and freshly ground black pepper

Heat the oil in a large saucepan and add the finely sliced onions. Cook for 3–5 minutes, stirring occasionally, till the onions are soft and transparent-looking, then add the rest of the prepared vegetables and the garlic. Cook, stirring from time to time, for about 10 minutes, then pour in the stock. Season with salt and pepper, half-cover the pan with its lid and simmer the soup very gently for half an hour.

Either cool completely before storing the soup in the fridge – or freezing it – or keep it hot till you are ready to ladle it into soup plates or bowls. It really doesn't need anything in the way of a garnish, because the vegetables themselves are so good colourwise.

This soup has the added benefit of being so low in calories that it is a real bonus for those who, like me, are perpetually totting up their calory intake.

Potato and Leek Soup

This, if I am pushed to choose a favourite soup above all others, would have to come top of my list. I love it in all its different ways of making – cold and velvety-smooth in the hot summer evenings, with snipped chives stirred through, or hot and smooth on chilly evenings, or, as in this case, half smooth and half chunky, which I think makes it perfect Sunday supper food. Anyone who doesn't like either curry powder or celery must be reassured that although both feature in the list of ingredients for this, my version of leek and potato soup, they need not worry – neither is discernible as such, but both go to make a whole, as it were, flavour-wise.

SERVES 6

1 oz/28 g butter + 2 tbsp sunflower oil

1 onion, skinned and chopped

1 stick celery, washed and trimmed and very finely sliced

4 leeks – more if they are small – washed and trimmed, and sliced diagonally (because it

looks nicer) into thin strips

4 medium potatoes, peeled and diced neatly

1 tsp medium strength curry powder

2 pts/1.1 L good chicken or vegetable stock

Salt and freshly ground black pepper

Melt the butter and heat the oil in a saucepan and add the chopped onion. Cook for 2–3 minutes, till the onion is soft and transparent, then stir in the celery and leeks, and cook for a further few minutes. Add the diced potatoes, stir in the curry powder, cook all together for a minute or two, then pour in the stock.

Simmer very gently for 25 minutes. Cool, liquidize half the soup, return it to the saucepan with the remainder of the soup and stir all together well. Taste, and season with salt and pepper. If you like, just before serving stir through the soup 1–2 tablespoons finely chopped parsley.

This soup can be made in advance by two or three days and reheated to serve, or it can be frozen – thaw overnight.

Scrambled Eggs with Smoked Haddock and Grilled Tomatoes

For this delicious supper dish, the cooked smoked fish is flaked and stirred into the eggs as they scramble – that way the fish warms up as the eggs cook. The fish can be cooked and flaked in the morning for supper that evening, and the eggs can be beaten with the pepper, Tabasco sauce and milk, all ready to scramble 5 minutes before you eat. The pinch of powdered ginger sprinkled on each tomato before grilling adds an interest which enhances the smoked haddock and scrambled eggs.

This is even better when served with toasted Cheese, Mustard and Garlic Granary Bread.

SERVES 6

12 tomatoes	*12 large eggs*
Butter	*¹/₄ pt/140 ml milk*
Powdered ginger	*A pinch of salt and plenty of*
A little sugar	*freshly ground black*
Salt and ground black	*pepper*
pepper	*A shake of Tabasco sauce*
1 lb/450 smoked haddock	
1 pt/570 ml milk and water	
mixed	

Wash the tomatoes, cut them in half and put the halves on a metal tray, with a tiny piece of butter on each and a pinch of powdered ginger, a pinch of sugar, one of salt, and a grinding of black pepper. This can be done as much as a day in advance, and the tray covered and left in a cool place.

Put the fish in a large pan and pour over the milk and water. Heat gently till a skin forms on the liquid, then take it off the heat. The fish will go on cooking as the liquid cools. When cool, flake the fish into a bowl, removing all skin and bones.

Beat the eggs with the milk, salt (not more than a pinch or two, the fish is quite salty), pepper and Tabasco sauce.

When you are almost ready to eat, begin to grill the tomatoes – they should be cooked until their skins are falling away. Melt the butter in a large saucepan – preferably a non-stick pan, for ease of washing up afterwards. Add the beaten eggs mixture and cook it over a gentle heat, scraping the bottom of the pan as you stir occasionally with a wooden spoon. The secret of scrambling eggs, I'm convinced, is to cook them slowly. As the mixture begins to scramble, stir in the flaked smoked haddock. Take the saucepan off the heat as soon as the eggs are creamily solid – they will continue to cook for a minute or two after the pan is taken off the heat, and overcooked scrambled eggs take on an unpleasant rubbery texture.

Serve, dividing the eggs between six warmed plates, with the grilled tomatoes, and toast and butter.

Black Pudding with Baked Apples

This just couldn't be simpler, but it is delicious and such a perfect supper dish for a Sunday night. Of course, it does all depend on the black pudding, it varies so much. There are three butchers who make the most superb black puddings. One is in Stornoway, one is in Lochcarron, and the third is MacBeth the butcher in Forres, who also mails his black puddings (and other meat and game) anywhere in the country. What I love about all these particular black puddings is that none of them is fatty – a fault found in most other types of black pud. The MacBeth's one is especially spicy, and in all three the oatmeal is distinctly discernible. I would be hard put to choose which of three is my favourite. I love each one. Grilled or, if you have an Aga or a Raeburn, baked in the hot oven with apples, black puddings make such ideal Sunday supper eating.

SERVES 6

12 slices of black pudding, each approx. ½ in/1 cm thick

*6 good eating apples, **never** dreary Golden Delicious, but ideally Cox's, washed, and scored*

around their middles, and with the core cut out – take care to feel with a finger and remove any of what Godfrey calls the 'toenail' bits of core

Put the black pudding slices either under a grill for 3–5 minutes each side, or in a hot oven, turning the slices over, and cooking them till they sizzle on top. At the same time, put the prepared apples into an ovenproof dish, and bake in a moderate oven for 20 minutes.

Serve two slices of black pudding on each warmed plate, flanked by a baked apple. This is quite filling, so only the hungriest, or perhaps a growing boy, will need a third slice.

Mushroom Meringue

This is a recipe given me by an old friend of my parents and ourselves called Brigadier Ley. He is the greatest cook and gourmet I know, and I love getting together with him, whenever I have a chance to pop down to my parents, and having a natter about recipes. He is an endless source of inspiration, and I always come back to Skye after a 'fix' of Hugh Ley's enthusiasm for matters culinary full of ideas for new dishes. This Mushroom Meringue is supposed to be a savoury, but I think that, given in more generous quantities than the original recipe, it makes a delicious Sunday night supper.

SERVES 6

---

6 slices of bread
Melted butter
2 tbsp sunflower oil and 2 oz/56 g butter
1 lb/450 g mushrooms, each wiped and chopped quite small
1 clove of garlic, skinned and finely chopped

A small carton (¹/₄ pt/140 ml) double cream beaten with 1 whole egg + 2 egg yolks
Salt and freshly ground black pepper
A grating of nutmeg
2 egg whites
6 oz/170 g Cheddar cheese, grated

Cut the crusts off the bread, brush each side of each slice with melted butter, and toast each side under a hot grill till golden brown. Have six plates warmed, and put a slice of toasted buttered bread on each plate.

Heat the oil and butter together in a non-stick frying pan and, when very hot, add the chopped mushrooms. Cooking them over a high heat helps to prevent their liquid from seeping out. Cook them with the chopped garlic till the mushrooms are almost crisp. Then take the pan off the heat and mix in the cream and egg mixture, seasoning it well first. Spread this mushroom mixture on top of each piece of toasted bread.

Whisk the egg whites till stiff. Scatter a little grated cheese on top of the mushrooms, spread each toast with a thin layer of egg white, and scatter the remainder of the grated cheese over the top.

Bake in a moderate oven, 350°F/180°C/Gas Mark 4, for 7–8 minutes. Serve immediately.

Eggs Benedict

This is really the most luxurious of suppers for a Sunday evening. I first ate Eggs Benedict in New Orleans in 1967, and I've been addicted to the dish ever since. For me, though, proper Eggs Benedict must have toasted muffins as their base – nothing else will do. But these days muffins are easy to find in good supermarkets, and they just need to be split and toasted. I allow one muffin, i.e. two halves, and two eggs, per person.

SERVES 6

6 muffins, split and toasted
12 small slices of ham, or 6
*   larger ones, each cut in*
*   half to fit the muffins*
12 poached eggs, or 12
*   softboiled eggs*

For the hollandaise sauce:
4 large egg yolks
¼ pt/140 ml wine vinegar
A slice of raw onion
A few crushed parsley stalks
A few black peppercorns
8 oz/225 g butter

Lightly butter the toasted muffins and cover each with a slice of ham.

If you prefer to softboil the eggs – when I say soft, I mean as opposed to hardboil – simmer them for 4 minutes, run cold water through the pan, and shell them carefully. Put an egg on top of each ham slice.

Simmer the vinegar in a pan with the onion, parsley stalks and peppercorns till it has reduced by more than half. Put the egg yolks in a food processor, melt the butter till very hot and then add it to the egg yolks in a steady thin stream, whizzing continuously. Lastly, strain the hot reduced vinegar into the hollandaise.

Put the muffin halves in a big serving dish and divide the hollandaise between them, spooning it over the eggs. If you like, flash the dish under a hot grill for just a second – but the eggs should still be hot, and the sauce fairly hot too, so if you prefer, just serve the eggs immediately.

Baked Eggs on Chopped Ham, Mushrooms and Garlic

Baked eggs make such a good supper dish for a Sunday evening. The ham and mushroom bit can be made the day before, and all you need to do before supper is to break the eggs on top, add a bit of butter and pop the ramekins in the oven. You do need quite big ramekins, or alternatively give two per person. These are good with the Sesame Toast on page 89 or with just plain toast.

SERVES 6

2 tbsp sunflower oil + 1 oz/ 28 g butter
½ lb/225 g mushrooms, wiped and chopped quite small
1 clove of garlic, skinned and finely chopped
6 oz/170 g baked ham

6 large eggs
A pinch of salt and plenty of freshly ground black pepper
Either 6 pieces of butter, each about 1 oz/28 g, or 6 tbsp cream

Butter six large ramekins.

Heat the oil and melt the butter in a frying pan and over a high heat cook the mushrooms and garlic together, cooking them till the mushrooms are almost crisp. Spoon them into the ramekins, dividing them evenly between the six. Chop the ham into small dice, and when the mushroom mixture is cool, spoon the chopped ham on top.

Before cooking time, break an egg into each ramekin on top of the ham and mushroom mixture, and put a pinch of salt and a grinding of black pepper on each. Put either a bit of butter or a spoonful of cream on each egg.

Bake in a moderate oven, 350°F/180°C/Gas Mark 4, till the eggs just wobble when you gently shake the ramekins. This takes about 7–10 minutes, depending on your oven. They will go on cooking for a few minutes once you have taken them out of the oven. Serve as soon as you can.

Chive and Tomato Omelette with Cottage Cheese

It really isn't very practical to plan omelettes for supper for much more than four people, because it means either eating in relays, or, if you eat all at the same time, the last omelette made is perfectly delicious whilst the first and second, which have been keeping warm, are inevitably rather less than perfect! But omelettes for a few people are delicious, and all the preparation can be done several hours ahead. In this case, the tomatoes can be skinned, de-seeded and chopped the previous day, and the chives snipped into the eggs, beaten all ready to be poured into the foaming butter in your omelette pan.

This type of omelette is particularly good with Black Olive, Sun-Dried Tomato and Garlic Bread (page 72) as an accompaniment.

SERVES 4

---

8 large eggs beaten together in a large jug with 4 tbsp cold water, ½ tsp salt, plenty of freshly ground black pepper and 4 tbsp snipped chives

Butter for the omelette pan
8 oz/225 g cottage cheese
6 tomatoes, skinned, de-seeded and chopped into small dice

If you beat the eggs in advance, you do need to fork through the mixture before making each omelette, to keep the snipped chives evenly distributed throughout.

To make each omelette, put a piece of butter in your omelette pan and swirl it around till it is hot and foaming, then, tipping and tilting the pan, pour in about a quarter of the mixture. The tipping and tilting distributes the mixture evenly over the base of the pan. Let it cook, lifting up the edges of the omelette to let the mixture run underneath, and just before it is cooked, while it is still slightly runny on top, spoon on a quarter of the cottage cheese, spreading it over the surface, and scatter a quarter of the diced tomatoes over that. Slip the cooked omelette on to a warm plate and repeat the process.

Welsh Rarebit

A lot of people think that Welsh rarebit is just melted cheese on toast – the cheese melted under a grill. But there is a lot more to a true Welsh Rarebit than that. It makes such a good supper, and is convenient in that the cheese mixture can be prepared ahead.

It's good with a salad of chopped apples and celery and walnuts, the flavours all combining very well with the cheese.

SERVES 4

1 tsp mustard powder	*2 beaten eggs*
¼ pt/140 ml dry cider	*4 muffins, split and toasted*
8 oz/225 g Cheddar cheese,	
grated	

Mix the mustard with the cider in a saucepan and stir in the grated cheese. Heat gently till the cheese has melted, then beat in the eggs.

Just before you want to eat, heat the grill, divide the cheese mixture between the toasted muffins, and grill till they are turning brown and are slightly puffy. Eat immediately.

Herring Roes
with Sesame Toast and Grilled Bacon

Herring roes are not readily found, but when they are, seize the chance and buy as much as you can eat for several days, never mind only Sunday suppers! They are best eaten with bacon, especially I think smoked bacon – the flavour of both smoked and unsmoked bacon goes so very well with all things fishy, and this is no exception. The Sesame Toast adds a good crisp and crunchy texture to the whole. The toast can be made ahead, and warmed up, if it's more convenient for you.

SERVES 6

12 rashers of smoked back bacon, grilled to the degree that you like
2 oz/56 g butter + 1 tbsp sunflower oil
1¹/₂ lb/675 g herring roes

For the toast:
6 slices of bread, brown or white, crusts cut off
3 oz/84 g butter, melted
6 tbsp sesame seeds mixed with 1 tsp salt

Melt the butter and heat the oil in a large pan, and gently fry the herring roes until firm.

Brush each slice of bread with melted butter, on each side. Press the salted sesame seeds into each buttered side, and toast under a hot grill, till the slices are golden brown on each side. If you prefer, before toasting you can cut the bread into strips, about three per slice.

Arrange roes, bacon and toast on six plates or a warm serving dish.

Rice in Chicken Stock
with Mushrooms and Garlic

This is one of those dishes which is so simple it almost precludes my telling you about it. On the other hand, it is just so good to eat, so quick and simple to make, that it justifies its presence in this chapter for those very reasons. If you have some good chicken stock to hand, it will be very much nicer than if you make it using a cube and water, but if you use Kallo stock cubes, which have no beastly monosodium glutamate and do actually taste good, that would be a good substitute.

SERVES 6

2 pts/1.1 L at least of
*   chicken stock*
12 oz/285 g Basmati rice
1 lb/450 g mushrooms,
*   wiped and chopped quite*
*   small*
1–2 cloves of garlic,
*   skinned and very finely*
*   chopped*

Salt and freshly ground
*   black pepper*
About 3 tbsp finely chopped
*   parsley*
Freshly grated Parmesan
*   cheese*

Put the stock into a large saucepan and bring to simmering point, then stir in the rice. Bring back to simmering point, stirring, and add the chopped mushrooms and the garlic. Simmer gently till the rice is cooked, about 10 minutes. Taste, and add salt and pepper to your taste.

Just before ladling this soupy mixture into soup plates, stir the chopped parsley through. Hand around the Parmesan in a bowl, for everyone to help themselves.

Camembert and Bacon Omelette

As with the Chive and Tomato Omelette with Cottage Cheese recipe (page 87), the two flavourings for this omelette, the bacon and the Camembert, can be prepared in the morning so that before supper all you need to do is to actually cook the omelettes. The bacon can be grilled, then chopped into small bits, and the rind can be cut off the Camembert and the cheese sliced into thin strips. The eggs can be beaten together, and the parsley chopped, so all that remains to be done is to put everything together.

SERVES 4

Butter for cooking the omelettes
8 large eggs beaten in a large jug with 4 tbsp water, salt, freshly ground black pepper and 2 tbsp finely chopped parsley

8 oz/225 g Camembert, rind sliced off and the cheese cut into strips
8 rashers of bacon, smoked or unsmoked, whichever you prefer, grilled and then chopped into small bits

Put a small piece of butter into your omelette pan over heat, and swirl it around till it is foaming. Pour in a quarter of the beaten eggs mixture, and as it swirls around so it will line the base of the omelette pan. Let it cook, lifting up the sides and letting the runny mixture slip underneath to cook. Lay the strips of Camembert on top of the omelette, a quarter of the amount, and scatter the same amount – a quarter – of the chopped bacon over. When the surface is just beginning to melt the cheese, slip the cooked omelette on to a warmed plate and fold it over. Repeat the process.

Children's Suppers

Mushroom Risotto

Kedgeree

Baked Potatoes with Tunafish and Sweetcorn Mayonnaise

Fish Cakes

Pasta with Tunafish and Chives

Sausagemeat and Apple Pie

Leek, Cheese and Crispy Bacon Lasagne

Smoked Cod (or Haddock) and Cheese Baked Pasta

Homemade Hamburgers

Chicken and Smoked Bacon Lasagne

Spinach and Sweetcorn Fritters

Sausages in Tomato and Garlic Sauce

Pizza

Onion, Mushroom and Sausage Toad-in-the-Hole

Cheese and Bacon Cauliflower

Frankfurter Casserole

Potato and Onion Pancakes

Cheese and Potato Stuffed Baked Tomatoes

CHILDREN'S SUPPERS

There are children I dread having to stay – those who will blench at the sight of anything other than a sausage or a fish finger. Although children can't be expected to like, for instance, the taste of a hot curry, most children will try – and enjoy – just about everything else, with a little encouragement and the odd bribe. I tried to make mine eat a tiny amount of things they didn't like just so that when they were guests in the homes of friends they would be able to eat more or less everything. And it's paid off. Hugo, who loathed peas, carrots and tomatoes, now loves all three. But then from an early age he loved Stilton and squid, so perhaps he isn't an ideal example! But I find that a way to get around fussy eating children is to get them to help in the preparation and cooking wherever possible – they love to eat something if they have had a hand in its making.

This chapter contains food which not only our children enjoy, but which also, for the most part, is 'safe' food for visiting children. Pasta seems to be universally popular. It is very convenient, too, when it can be made up into a complete supper, as in the recipe for Leek, Cheese and Crispy Bacon Lasagne. Hamburgers, which we usually make to barbecue (how I love the taste of charcoal-grilled food) are very much nicer when made at home – I make my own mince, that way I know what has gone into it. And the Spinach and Sweetcorn Fritters are requested frequently here during the holidays. I realize that dishes like Kedgeree depend on the children liking fish, but as ours do, so, I suppose, must others. And Baked Potatoes with Tunafish and Sweetcorn Mayonnaise should probably come top of the list of favourite suppers – in our home, anyway!

Mushroom Risotto

This is a top favourite supper with each one of the six of us – with other dishes there are invariably one or two of the family who are lukewarm in their enthusiasm, but for Mushroom Risotto and for most pasta recipes we are as one in our appreciation for them.

Good risotto needs good stock. You *can* use a cube and water but proper good stock makes all the difference in the world. It is also so important to cook the rice for several minutes in the olive oil with the onions, garlic and mushrooms so that each grain becomes coated in oil, and then the stock and dry white wine must be added in small amounts, and the rice stirred slowly with a wooden spoon from time to time. The rice will absorb the liquid as it simmers gently.

If you, like us, pick your own wild mushrooms you can chop those and use them instead of the cultivated mushrooms. Add the chopped parsley at the very last minute before serving.

SERVES 6

4–5 tbsp extra virgin olive oil

2 onions, skinned and finely chopped

1–2 cloves of garlic, skinned and finely chopped

1 lb/450 g mushrooms, wiped and chopped

About 1 lb/450 g Arborio rice

¼ pt/140 ml dry white wine

2–2½ pts/1.1–1.4 L good chicken or vegetable stock

Salt and plenty of freshly ground black pepper

2–3 tbsp finely chopped parsley

Freshly grated Parmesan cheese, to hand around with the risotto

---

Heat the oil in a wide sauté pan and add the chopped onions. Cook till they are soft and transparent, then add the garlic and mushrooms and cook them for a couple of minutes before stirring in the rice. Cook, stirring gently, for a couple of minutes, then pour in the wine. Simmer very gently, and when the wine is almost absorbed, add a small amount of the stock. Simmer gently and when the stock is almost absorbed, add more. Continue till the stock is used, and stir in the salt, pepper and parsley just before serving.

Kedgeree

Because this is a rice-based dish, it is a great favourite with our children as well as with Godfrey and me. If you think children tend not to like eating fish, it is usually not the taste as much as the fear of finding bones in any fishy dish. You can assure them they won't find a bone, in all honesty, if you feel the raw fish with your fingertips before you cook it and cut out or pull out any bones you feel – they are much harder to remove once the fish is cooked, and very difficult to see.

I like Kedgeree best when it is made with smoked haddock or cod – and I really prefer smoked cod, with the large juicy flakes of fish. I cook the rice in the milk-and-water liquid the fish cooked in. Proper Kedgeree has sultanas in it – I leave them out, because two of our children dislike them so much. I do, on the other hand, cook a teaspoon of medium strength curry powder in the butter and oil when I sauté the chopped onions. This, and the chopped parsley stirred through the Kedgeree just before dishing up, really makes a delicious dish.

All you need is a salad of grated carrots or mixed salad leaves to accompany the buttery Kedgeree.

SERVES 6

1½ lb/675 g smoked haddock or cod	*12 oz/340 g long grain rice*
	The strained fish liquid
1 pt/570 ml milk + 1 pt/570 ml water	*3 hardboiled eggs, shelled and chopped*
2 tbsp sunflower oil + 1 oz/ 28 g butter	*3 oz/84 g butter, cut in bits*
	Lots of freshly ground black pepper
2 medium onions, skinned and finely chopped	*2 tbsp chopped parsley*
1 tsp medium strength curry powder	

Feel the fish with your fingertips and remove all bones. Put the fish into a saucepan with the milk and water, and heat gently till the liquid forms a skin and just begins to simmer. Take the pan off the heat and leave to cool completely. When cooled, strain the liquid into a jug, and flake the fish into a bowl, removing all skin.

Heat the oil and melt the ounce of butter together in a saucepan and add the finely chopped onions. Cook for several minutes till they are soft and transparent-looking, then stir in the curry powder. Stir in the rice, and cook for several minutes till the rice is coated on each grain with oil. Pour in the liquid till it comes an inch/2.5 cm above the rice – you need to take the pan off the heat to do this, as the heat initially will create a lot of steam that makes it impossible to see the depth of liquid till the heat lowers. Don't stir once the liquid is added, but replace the pan on the heat, cover the pan with a folded teatowel, then with the lid of the pan, and cook gently on moderate heat for 5 minutes. Then take the pan off the heat and leave, covered, for 15 minutes. By this time the liquid should be completely absorbed by the rice.

Stir in the flaked fish – I use a fork to do this – and the chopped hardboiled eggs and the bits of butter. Season with black pepper – the fish will be sufficiently salty so there is no need to add salt. Just before serving, fork through the chopped parsley.

Baked Potatoes with Tunafish and Sweetcorn Mayonnaise

This must surely be one of the easiest suppers, but it is certainly the supper made most often by our children when left to their own devices in the kitchen. It is very filling, and very convenient too, in that the tunafish and sweetcorn mayonnaise can all be mixed together and left, in a covered bowl in the fridge, several hours before supper. The potatoes can be scrubbed and stabbed through to help them cook more quickly and to prevent them from bursting during cooking. All that is needed is to remember to put the potatoes into the oven. If you want to inject some vitamin C, get the children to add a couple of tablespoons of chopped parsley to the tunafish mixture – this perks up the colour, and children are great ones for the visually appealing, so this is usually a good move.

SERVES 6

6 good-sized potatoes for baking
For the filling:
6 tbsp mayonnaise
A 15-oz/420-g tin of sweetcorn kernels, drained of their brine

Two 6½-oz/185-g tins of flaked tunafish in either oil or brine – drain off whichever
2 tbsp finely chopped parsley

Scrub the potatoes under running water. Dry them, and rub with a very small amount of oil, then roll each potato in rock salt – this is optional. Put them on a baking tray, and stick a knife right through each potato. Bake in a hot oven, 42°F/220°C/Gas Mark 7, for about 45 minutes – you may need longer if the potatoes are huge. With oven gloves on, gently squeeze the largest potato. When it feels soft the potatoes are cooked. Take them out of the oven and serve each on a plate and split open.

Mix together the mayonnaise, drained sweetcorn, drained flaked tuna and parsley. Serve in a bowl with the baked potatoes.

Fish Cakes

These are very different from the bought type of fish cake, which is bright orange because of its coating, and which consists of vastly more potato than fish. I only ever make Fish Cakes using smoked haddock or cod, because their flavour is so much better. Whether it is their flavour, or their crispy coating once fried, I don't know, but they are tremendously popular with not only our children but all visiting children. My only problem is actually having enough.

I like to serve these fish cakes with a tomatoey sauce, and a vegetable such as peas cooked with sautéed onions and garnished with crispy bits of bacon – bacon complements the taste of all fish and shellfish.

SERVES 6

2 lb/900 g smoked haddock or cod	*2 tbsp each finely chopped parsley and snipped chives*
Milk to cook the fish	
2 lb/900 g potatoes, peeled, cut in half and boiled till cooked	*2 eggs, beaten in a shallow dish*
Freshly ground black pepper	*About 4 oz/112 g brown breadcrumbs*
	Sunflower oil for frying

Feel the fish with your fingertips and remove all bones. Put the fish into a saucepan with milk to cover, and cook till the milk just simmers. Take the pan off the heat and let the fish cool in the milk. Then strain off the milk into a jug.

Flake the fish, removing all skin. Mash the cooked and drained potatoes well, adding a small amount of the fish milk (keep the rest for soup) and beat in the flaked fish. Beat in the pepper, parsley and chives.

Dip your hands in flour, and shape the fish and potato mixture into cakes, dipping each in beaten egg then on either side into the breadcrumbs. This is a messy procedure, and one in which children love to help for that very reason. As the cakes are shaped and coated, put them on a baking tray lined with greaseproof paper.

Either freeze them at this stage, or put them in the fridge. Fry them till golden brown on each side in a small amount of oil, and butter too, if you like. Drain on absorbent kitchen paper on a warm serving dish.

Pasta with Tunafish and Chives

This is a quick and easy pasta sauce that tastes delicious. It can be made by child or adult – our children would eat tunafish with anything, so this is often made by them. If you can't lay your hands on chives, you can substitute snipped top ends of spring onions.

SERVES 6

2 oz/56 g butter
1 tbsp flour
1¹/₂ pts/850 ml milk, or, if you like, 1 pt/570 ml milk and ¹/₂ pt/285 ml single cream
Salt and pepper

Two 6¹/₂-oz/185-g tins tunafish, drained of oil or brine
3 oz/84 g Cheddar cheese, grated
2 tbsp snipped chives
3 oz/84 g pasta per person
2 tbsp sunflower oil, or olive oil

Melt the butter in a saucepan and stir in the flour. Cook for a minute, then gradually add the milk, a little at a time, stirring continuously. If you use a wire whisk to do this you will get a really smooth sauce without the danger of lumps forming in the sauce. Once the sauce boils it is impossible to break down any lumps, so take care when stirring and adding the milk not to let this happen. Once all the milk is added let the sauce boil, still stirring, and then take the pan off the heat. Don't worry, the sauce will be runny. Season with salt and pepper, and stir in the flaked drained tunafish and the grated cheese. Stir in the chives.

Boil the pasta in a large saucepan with plenty of salted boiling water. Boil till you can stick the prongs of a fork into a bit of pasta. Then put a colander in the sink and pour the contents of the saucepan into the colander. When drained, put the pasta back in its pan and toss it with a couple of tablespoons of either sunflower or olive oil.

Serve immediately, spooned on to plates, with a ladleful of sauce on each helping of pasta.

Sausagemeat and Apple Pie

This is one of those invaluable dishes which freezes well, is an entire meal in one dish, and tastes delicious. The idea was my sister Livi's many years ago. I think it matters very much whenever sausages or sausagemeat is used in a recipe to get the very best you can find – I like Marks & Spencer's butcher style or free-range sausages, or their Lincoln sausages. I much prefer to skin my own, and this is a task which Hugo loves doing. The sausages just need to be slit down with a sharp knife and the skins peel off easily.

The chopped apples in this pie go very well with the sausage-meat, and the sautéed chopped onions and the thyme just make all the flavours set each other off perfectly. I like to beat chopped parsley and snipped chives or very finely chopped garlic into the well-beaten mashed potatoes for the top of the pie.

SERVES 6

---

3 tbsp sunflower oil

2 medium onions, skinned and finely chopped

1–2 cloves of garlic, skinned and very finely chopped

3 tart eating apples – Granny Smith's are ideal for this (or Cox's)

2 lb/900 g top-quality pork sausages, each slit and skinned

2 tbsp tomato purée

1 tbsp flour

A good pinch of thyme

¹/₂ pt/285 ml dry apple juice (with no sweetener)

¹/₂ pt/285 ml chicken or vegetable stock

Salt and freshly ground black pepper

About 1¹/₂ lb/675 g well-beaten mashed potatoes containing chopped parsley and snipped chives – beating with a wooden spoon gives a very creamy texture to mashed potatoes

Butter for the topping

Heat the oil in a heavy saucepan or casserole dish and cook the chopped onions till they are soft and beginning to turn golden. Add the garlic and the chopped apples and cook for a few minutes, then scoop this mixture out into a bowl. Brown the sausagemeat, stirring all the time to break it up. When you have mashed it up as best you can, and it is browned, replace the onion-and-apple mixture in the pan. Stir in the tomato purée and the flour, and the thyme. Gradually stir in the apple juice and the stock, and stir till the mixture bubbles. Season with salt and pepper, and simmer very gently for 15 minutes, stirring from time to time to prevent the mixture from sticking. Pour into a pie dish and cool.

Cover with the beaten mashed potatoes, forking the surface into a neat pattern. Dot with tiny bits of butter and cook the pie in a moderate oven, 350°F/180°C/Gas Mark 4, for 30 minutes, till the potato is turning crisply golden on its forked pattern, and the filling is bubbling. If you put the pie directly from the fridge into the oven, you will need to add about 20 minutes on to the cooking time.

This is good served with cabbage.

Leek, Cheese and Crispy Bacon Lasagne

The leeks and cheese go together so well, and the crispy bacon is sprinkled over the surface doubling up both as a garnish and a different texture and also as a taste enhancer. Another meal in one dish, my ideal, and a dish which can be put together easily if not by you, then by a fairly competent child – by this I mean one that will wash up properly after the making is finished!

SERVES 6

2 oz/56 g butter + 2 tbsp sunflower oil

12 medium to large leeks, each washed well and trimmed, and sliced

neatly into ¼-in/½-cm bits

8 oz/225 g Cheddar cheese, grated – set aside about a third of this

Salt and pepper

A grating of nutmeg
1 clove of garlic, skinned
and finely chopped
2 oz/56 g flour
2 pts/1.1 l milk

About 12 sheets of lasagne –
I like to use the green
type for this
12 rashers of smoked
streaky bacon, grilled till
crisp, then broken up

Butter a shallow ovenproof dish. Melt the butter in a saucepan and add the sunflower oil. Cook the sliced leeks in this till the leeks are really soft. This doesn't take very long if you use a fairly wide pan – a sauté pan is ideal. Then add the chopped garlic and stir in the flour. Cook for a minute, then gradually add the milk, stirring continuously till the sauce boils. The sauce will be quite runny, but it is meant to be – the pasta absorbs a lot of milk as it cooks.

When the sauce has boiled, take the pan off the heat, stir in two-thirds of the grated cheese, and season with salt, pepper and nutmeg. Spoon some of the sauce over the base of the dish. Layer up the pasta and sauce, ending with the sauce. Sprinkle the rest of the grated cheese over the surface, and bake in a moderate oven, 350°F/180°C/Gas Mark 4, for about 25–30 minutes, till the pasta feels soft when you stick a fork in it. The cheese on top should be golden brown.

Sprinkle the broken-up bacon evenly over the surface.

Smoked Cod (or Haddock) and Cheese Baked Pasta

This is just a variation on a fish pie (one of my favourite dishes) which came to mind (and then to table) when our third daughter, Meriel, went through a phase of not liking potato-topped pies. It's rather good, and very simple to make.

You can use either smoked cod or smoked haddock, but I prefer to use cod because of the large and juicy flakes of fish. It's good with a tomato salad to go with it. I use pasta shells or bows for this dish.

SERVES 6

---

2 lb/900 g smoked haddock or cod – feel for bones with your fingers, and cut them out of the fish before cooking	*2 oz/56 g flour*
	2 pts/1.1 L of the milk in which the fish cooked
	6 oz/170g Cheddar cheese, grated
2 pts/1.1 L milk	*Ground black pepper*
2 oz/56 g butter	*12 oz/340 g pasta*
1 onion, skinned and finely chopped	*2 tbsp finely chopped parsley*

Put the fish into a saucepan with the milk and over a moderate heat, bring it to a gentle simmer. Take the pan off the heat and let the fish cool in the milk. Then strain the milk into a jug and flake the fish, removing all skin.

Melt the butter in a saucepan and cook the finely chopped onion in the butter till the onion is soft and transparent-looking. Stir in the flour, cook for a minute, then gradually stir in the strained fish milk, stirring all the time till the sauce boils. Take the pan off the heat, stir in about two-thirds of the grated cheese, and season with black pepper. Stir in the flaked fish.

Meanwhile, cook the pasta in plenty of boiling salted water till soft – about 8 minutes. Drain, and mix into the smoked fish and cheesy sauce. Pour into a buttered pie dish and scatter the rest of the grated cheese over the top. Grill till the cheese has melted, then scatter the chopped parsley over, and serve.

Homemade Hamburgers

I have a horror of bought hamburgers, because unless I know the butcher who made them, I don't know what has gone into them. I much prefer to make my own, by buying good meat and pulverizing it in my food processor. I like to make it quite chunky, rather than smooth. You do need a bit of fat to make the hamburgers juicy. I also like to add sautéed onions to the mixture, and an egg, and a dash of Worcestershire sauce. I find that children like to have a – clean – hand in making the hamburgers, and they do taste good when cooked on a barbecue – I love the taste of charcoal-grilled food.

All that is needed to go with them is a lot of tomato ketchup, but only Heinz will do, buttered buns, salad and a bowl of potato crisps. And a lot of paper table napkins (or absorbent kitchen paper) to mop up.

SERVES 6 – 2 HAMBURGERS PER PERSON

2 lb/900 g fairly lean steak – *I use rump*	*2 tbsp sunflower oil*
	1 egg
2 onions, skinned and very *finely chopped*	*1 tbsp Worcestershire sauce*
	Ground black pepper

Trim any gristle from the meat, but try to leave some fat on. Cut the meat into bits and put it into the food processor. Cook the chopped onions in the sunflower oil till they are soft, then cool them. Add them to the meat, and whiz, taking care not to let the meat become too smooth. Add the egg, Worcestershire sauce and pepper to the contents of the processor and whiz briefly to amalgamate the lot.

Shape twelve hamburgers and put them on a tray lined with greaseproof paper, cover them with clingfilm and put them into the fridge till you are ready to barbecue them. Those wire containers (see page 50) are invaluable for barbecuing, because you can cook several hamburgers at once and turn them all over at the same time, but I find they come off the mesh much more easily if I brush it with oil before putting the hamburgers on.

Chicken and Smoked Bacon Lasagne

In this recipe I whiz the raw chicken with the streaky bacon in a food processor. This is best done a small amount at a time. It is made into a sauce with mushrooms and garlic, and it does seem to go down very well with children as well as adults.

It needs only a crunchy salad of shredded cabbage and grated carrots, or a plain green salad, to go with it.

SERVES 6

---

8 chicken breasts

8 rashers of smoked streaky bacon

2 oz/56 g butter and 2 tbsp sunflower oil

1 onion, skinned and finely chopped

1–2 cloves of garlic, skinned and very finely chopped

1/2 lb/225 g mushrooms, wiped and chopped

2 oz/56 g flour

2 pts/1.1 L milk

Salt and ground black pepper

12 sheets of green lasagne (the green makes the result look more interesting)

3 oz/84 g Cheddar cheese, grated

Slice the chicken into bits, removing any skin and bone. Put the bits into the food processor with the bacon, cut into 1-inch/2.5-cm lengths. Whiz together briefly to just chop them, rather than to pulverize.

Heat the oil and melt the butter together in a wide saucepan – a sauté pan – and brown the chicken and bacon mixture, mashing it with a wooden spoon to break it up. As it browns, remove it to a dish to keep warm. Then cook the chopped onion and the garlic, till the onion is soft and just beginning to turn colour. Add the mushrooms, and almost immediately stir in the flour. Gradually add the milk, stirring all the time till the sauce boils. Take the pan off the heat, stir in the browned chicken and bacon mixture, and season with salt and pepper.

Spoon some of this sauce over the base of a buttered ovenproof dish. Cover with a layer of pasta, then cover this with more sauce. Continue layering up the pasta and sauce, ending with sauce. The sauce will be rather runny but don't worry – the pasta absorbs a lot of liquid as it cooks. Scatter the grated cheese over the surface.

Bake in a moderate oven, 350°F/180°C/Gas Mark 4, for about 30 minutes, till when you stick a fork in the middle the pasta feels soft. The cheese will be golden brown. Serve as soon as possible.

Spinach and Sweetcorn Fritters

I think it is a fallacy that children don't like eating spinach. These fritters are winners, and they can either be a supper by themselves, with perhaps a tomato sauce, or they can be served with sausages or bacon. They are quite filling, and you can include the garlic or not, as you like. I do!

SERVES 6

4 oz/112 g plain flour	*spinach, thawed, drained*
2 large eggs	*well and chopped*
Salt and pepper	*1 clove of garlic, skinned*
2 lb/900 g fresh spinach,	*and finely chopped*
steamed till it just wilts,	*Two 15-oz/420-g tins of*
then chopped quite	*sweetcorn kernels,*
finely, or ½ lb frozen	*drained of their brine*
leaf	

Beat together the flour and eggs, and season them with the salt and pepper. Beat in the well-chopped spinach, the finely chopped garlic and the sweetcorn. Lightly oil a non-stick frying pan or, if you have an Aga or a Raeburn, lightly oil the cooler hotplate and drop on spoonfuls of the mixture, well spaced out. After a minute or so, turn them over – I use a palate knife to do this. When they are golden brown (well flecked with the green spinach), pile them on to a warmed serving plate or dish and eat as soon as possible.

Sausages in Tomato and Garlic Sauce

Sausages can be made into a much more interesting supper with very little extra effort beyond just grilling them. In this recipe the sausages are grilled, because I personally loathe the look of anaemic sausages, however well cooked they are, and they are, in the tomatoey sauce. I much prefer browned pieces of sausage. As with all recipes using sausages, it is vital to buy really good sausages, those which state on the package that they contain a high percentage of pork meat.

This is good with baked potatoes and a salad.

SERVES 6

3 tbsp olive oil	Two 15-oz/420-g tins of
2 medium onions, skinned and finely chopped	chopped tomatoes
1 stick of celery, washed, trimmed and very finely sliced	Salt and freshly ground black pepper
	A pinch of sugar
1–2 cloves of garlic, skinned and very finely chopped	2 lb/900 g best pork sausages, grilled till browned, then cut into 1-in/2.5-cm bits

Heat the olive oil and add the finely chopped onions and sliced celery, and cook them till the onions are turning golden. Then add the garlic, and the tins of tomatoes. Season with salt, pepper and sugar, and simmer gently, with the pan uncovered, for 30 minutes. Stir in the sliced grilled sausages, simmer all together gently for a further 10 minutes, and serve. This dish keeps warm without spoiling for about half an hour in a low temperature oven.

Pizza

It isn't only children who love pizza – Godfrey and I do every bit as much as any of our four! But they do need to have a good surface covering (I loathe the word topping) of tomatoes, garlic, anchovies, cheese and black olives.

Whatever you use them in, and pizza is no exception, the quality of the olives matters. The ones I don't like to use are those preserved in brine, because they taste of the brine and not of olive. The ones I go for are those preserved with herbs, and once opened, I store any unused in oil.

Making pizza is so much easier now that we can buy the dough bases, but living where we do, we can't – yet – buy them in Skye. So I still have to make the base for pizza when I run out of the bought, which is why I give you the recipe I use. For the surface, if you don't like olives, or anchovies, or even garlic, just leave them out. And you may well find it more convenient to make a baking tray of pizza rather than the traditional round shape.

Try experimenting with the other possibilities for the surface – smoked fish, cream cheese (instead of mozzarella) and dill weed make a different and delicious Pizza, for a more special occasion.

SERVES 6

For the base:
1 lb/450 g strong plain white flour
½ pt/285 ml warm water containing 2 tsp sugar and 1 tbsp dried yeast stirred well into the

water; leave for about 15 minutes in a warm place till the yeast has developed a froth double the amount in size to the water

1–2 cloves of garlic, skinned and finely chopped
1 tsp salt
1 tbsp olive oil
For the content:
1 pt/570 ml homemade tomato sauce (see p.54)
1 lb/450 g good mozzarella cheese, cut into thin strips
1 tin anchovies, finely chopped – if you prefer

a less salty taste, soak them in milk for 10 minutes first, then drain well
As many good black olives as you like, stoned and chopped in half
Fresh basil leaves – optional – torn
Lots of freshly ground black pepper – no more salt, if you use anchovies

Mix the frothed-up yeast liquid into the flour with the chopped garlic, salt and olive oil. On a floured surface knead well till the dough feels pliant – smooth and not sticky, I count to 200 which seems to give about the right amount of kneading time! Oil two 9–10 inch/22–25 cm round tins and work the dough so that it covers the base of each – do this by dividing the dough between the tins and push it with the heel of your hand till it covers the bases.

Spread tomato sauce over each base. Distribute the strips of mozzarella, the chopped anchovies, halved olives and basil on top, and grind pepper over.

Bake in a very hot oven, 420°F/220°C/Gas Mark 7, for 10–15 minutes till the pizza base is golden brown at the edges and puffed up.

Onion, Mushroom and Sausage Toad-in-the-Hole

In this most favourite supper, there is a variation on the theme of the usual toad-in-the-hole – we think that the sautéed onions and mushrooms make it more interesting. I like to use chipolata sausages for making toad, but if you can't get good chipolatas, just use good ordinary-sized sausages, grilled and cut in half.

SERVES 6

6 oz/170 g flour sieved with a pinch of salt and plenty of freshly ground black pepper	*3 onions, skinned and finely sliced*
3 large eggs	*1–2 cloves of garlic, skinned and finely chopped*
½ pt/285 ml milk and water, mixed	*1 lb/450 g mushrooms, wiped and chopped*
3 tbsp sunflower oil	*1½ lb/675 g good pork chipolatas, grilled till golden brown*

Start by beating together, or putting into a food processor, the flour, eggs, milk and water. Cover the batter and leave to stand for half an hour.

In a saucepan heat the oil and cook the finely sliced onions till they are soft and just beginning to turn golden – about 5–8 minutes. Then add the chopped garlic and mushrooms and continue to cook, stirring to prevent them from sticking, over a high heat for several minutes. You may need to add another tablespoon or two of oil. Pour this mixture into a baking tin or deep tray – because the batter cooks much better than in pyrex or heatproof porcelain – and lay the grilled sausages on top. Pour the batter over the top.

Cook in a very hot oven, 420°F/220°C/Gas Mark 7, for about 30–35 minutes, till the top is well puffed up and dark golden in colour.

Serve with cabbage or broccoli.

Cheese and Bacon Cauliflower

This is a much more interesting version of cauliflower cheese. The
sauce can be made ahead and reheated to pour over the steamed or
boiled cauliflower, and it is very good served with baked potatoes –
the sauce is sufficiently rich to make butter with the potatoes
unnecessary, so I tell my children and Godfrey, who still manage
to sneak the butter dish on to the table!

SERVES 6

*2 oz/56 g butter + 1 tbsp
  sunflower oil*
*2 medium onions, skinned
  and finely sliced*
*1–2 cloves of garlic,
  skinned and finely
  chopped*
1 tsp French mustard
2 oz/56 g flour
1¼ pts/710 g milk
*6 oz/170 g Cheddar cheese,
  grated*
*Salt and freshly ground
  black pepper*

*2 medium cauliflowers,
  washed well, trimmed
  and cut into large
  florets; steam till just
  tender when you stick a
  fork in the thickest part
  of each stem – I loathe
  chewy cauliflower, but
  almost as bad is
  overcooked, mushy
  cauli!*
*8 rashers of smoked or
  unsmoked back bacon,
  grilled and chopped in
  bits*

Melt the butter and heat the oil together in a saucepan and add the
sliced onions. Cook till they are soft and just turning golden. Stir in
the chopped garlic, the mustard and flour, and cook for a minute,
then, stirring continuously, gradually add the milk, stirring till the
sauce boils. Take the pan off the heat and stir in the grated cheese,
all but a couple of tablespoons, and season well.

Put the steamed cauliflower into a warmed heatproof dish and
pour the sauce over it. Scatter the chopped bacon over the sauce,
and scatter the remaining grated cheese on top. Pop the dish under
a hot grill to melt the cheese, and serve.

Frankfurter Casserole

This recipe was given to me by an American friend, and it is perfect food for a group of children or teenagers. I love frankfurters – I buy the ones in Marks & Spencer which you boil in their foil container. This seems much more popular than chili con carne, certainly with our children and their friends. I like to use small cannellini beans and sweetcorn kernels, but you could substitute red kidney beans if you prefer.

It's good served with either baked potatoes, or warm French bread cut in chunks and garlic-buttered.

SERVES 6

---

3 tbsp olive oil
3 medium onions, skinned and quite finely chopped
1–2 cloves of garlic, skinned and finely chopped
Two 15-oz/420-g tins of chopped tomatoes
2 tbsp Heinz tomato ketchup
A pinch of salt, if you think it needs it, and ground black pepper

Two 15-oz/420-g tins of sweetcorn kernels, drained of their brine
Two 15-oz/420-g tins of cannellini beans, drained
2 lb/900 g frankfurters, steamed till cooked – usually 5 minutes – and cut in 1-in/2.5-cm chunks
3 oz/84 g Cheddar cheese, grated

Heat the oil in a saucepan and add the chopped onions. Cook for several minutes till the onions are soft and just turning golden. Stir in the chopped garlic and the chopped tomatoes, the ketchup and the pepper – then the salt if you think it needs it.

Simmer very gently for 5 minutes, then stir in the drained sweetcorn and drained cannellini beans and continue to simmer, gently, for 10 minutes. Pour into a heatproof dish and stir in the chopped frankfurters.

Sprinkle the grated cheese over the surface and grill till the cheese is melted and turning golden brown. Serve.

Potato and Onion Pancakes

Potato scones are delicious, but these, with sautéed chopped onion through the mixture, are just as good when served with crispy grilled streaky bacon and perhaps a green salad.

The flavouring of thyme in the mixture is optional, but I recommend it. If you use dried thyme, just a pinch will do – if the thyme is fresh, strip a stalk of its leaves.

SERVES 6

1¹/₂ lb/675g potatoes	*2 medium onions, skinned*
Salt and pepper	*and finely chopped*
2 oz/56 g butter	*1 clove garlic, skinned and*
A pinch of thyme	*finely chopped*
1 oz/28 g butter + 1 tbsp	*2 oz/56 g plain flour,*
sunflower oil	*sieved*
	2 eggs, beaten

Boil the potatoes till tender, drain them well and mash them. With a wooden spoon, beat in the salt, pepper, butter and thyme.

Melt the second portion of butter with the oil in a saucepan and cook the chopped onions till they are turning golden brown. Add the chopped garlic and cook for a further minute, then beat this mixture into the mashed potatoes. Beat in the sieved flour and the eggs.

Butter or oil a griddle, or the cool hotplate of an Aga or Raeburn. Make small flat cakes of the potato mixture and cook them on the oiled griddle for 2–3 minutes, turning them over halfway through the cooking time. Keep them warm till the mixture is all made up.

Cheese and
Potato Stuffed Baked Tomatoes

You really need the big 'beef' tomatoes for this recipe, although you can use ordinary-sized tomatoes, and have three per person. If you have fresh basil, all the better. The stuffing for this dish takes very little time to prepare – preparing the actual tomatoes takes about as long. But both can be done by a competent child, and they are so delicious that they are enjoyed by child and adult alike.

Perhaps just a salad is all that is needed to accompany these stuffed tomatoes – or a vegetable such as sautéed courgettes.

SERVES 6

12 beef tomatoes	*About 1½ lb/675 g leftover*
2 tbsp sunflower or olive oil	*boiled new or old potatoes, cut into large dice*
1 onion, skinned and finely chopped	*Salt and pepper*
1–2 cloves of garlic, skinned and finely chopped	*6 oz/170 g Cheddar cheese, grated*
	As much torn-up basil as you have available

Prepare the tomatoes by slicing off their stalk ends and, with a teaspoon, carefully scooping out their inner seeds – I say carefully because you don't want to tear the tomato at all. Leave the empty tomatoes cut side down on absorbent kitchen paper while you make the stuffing.

Heat the oil in a saucepan and cook the onion in it, adding the chopped garlic when the onion is soft and turning golden brown. Then stir in the diced potatoes, salt and pepper, and cook for a further few minutes. Mix in the grated cheese and torn basil, and take the pan off the heat. Put the tomatoes into an oiled heatproof dish, and divide the stuffing between each tomato.

Bake in a moderately hot oven, 350°F/180°C/Gas Mark 4, for 30 minutes.

High Teas

HIGH TEAS

High teas are distinguishable from children's suppers in that I always think that high teas should consist of the sort of food I would like to eat at breakfast-time – things like scrambled eggs with lots of crisply cooked bacon and grilled tomatoes, or kippers, or poached eggs on marmite-spread toast.

Of course, you can eat anything at all for high tea – as with any meal, you eat what you like to eat, not what I or anyone tells you you should be eating, so just because a high tea for me is breakfast-type food it doesn't mean that I think that is the only food you can serve at a high tea! In fact, quite a few of the recipes in the chapter on Children's Suppers would make good high tea food – things like Fish Cakes, or Cheese and Potato Stuffed Baked Tomatoes, or Spinach and Sweetcorn Fritters. But I think that I wouldn't really want to sit down to a meat and vegetable type of dish at high tea, because the other part of a high tea, for me at any rate, consists of buttered scones and jam, cakes and biscuits.

High tea is really a cross between an early supper and tea – just the thing if you are taking a group of children (or adults for that matter!) to a film or play, when you don't know whether to eat before or afterwards, but finally decide that your family and guests may be hungry with nothing. So you opt for high tea before, followed, perhaps, by hot soup afterwards.

Leftover Suppers and Storecupboard Suppers

Shepherd's Pie

Beef (or Lamb) Cakes

Devilled Tunafish

Pasta with Garlic, Olive Oil and Black Olives

Curried Eggs

Stuffed Egg Salad

Sautéed Chicken Livers with Onions, Apples and Cream

Cheese, Ham and Mushroom Puff Pastry Slice

Tomato and Onion Tart

Mango and Curried Chicken Salad

Avocado and Bacon Salad with Pinhead Oatmeal Bread

Tomato Cream Dressed Avocado Salad

LEFTOVER SUPPERS
AND STORECUPBOARD SUPPERS

The recipes in this chapter are mainly about the using-up necessary in all families – when there isn't quite enough leftover roast chicken, or roast lamb, or beef, to make a complete supper, so invention has to come into use to stretch the basic ingredient. Such dishes can be every bit as delicious as the original in its straight – usually roast – first appearance was.

Also there are one or two recipes for the panic supper when you may have thought no-one would be home for supper but you find there are suddenly mouths to feed, and you open your storecupboard desperately seeking inspiration from the contents. As long as you have both Arborio (risotto) and Basmati rice and plenty of pasta always in stock, you can't go too far wrong – a good bottle of olive oil, a jar of black olives, some freshly grated Parmesan cheese in the freezer, some dried mushrooms, and you have the where-withal for a fine impromptu supper without having to resort to a take-away (impossible where we live anyway) or tinned foods.

Not that there is anything wrong with tinned foods – a few tins of sardines in the cupboard, and I prefer the ones in oil to the ones in tomato sauce, make a good supper when they are mashed well with fromage frais and paprika, then heaped on toast and grilled for a few minutes. And provided you have plenty of eggs, you really are home and dry – no-one need go hungry!

Shepherd's Pie

This is one way to eke out leftover roast lamb – a proper shepherd's pie can only be made with lamb, although you can of course do variations on the theme using leftover beef or venison.

3 tbsp sunflower oil

2 onions, skinned and finely
    chopped

1–2 cloves of garlic, skinned
    and finely chopped

If you have any leftover
    gravy, use it up in this, if
    not:

1 tbsp flour – white or
    wholemeal

2 tbsp tomato purée

1¼ pts/710 ml lager and
    water mixed

Salt and ground black
    pepper

2 tbsp Worcestershire sauce

About 1½ lb/675 g leftover
    lamb, trimmed of fat and
    gristle (If there is less,
    just add more onions and
    even a tin of tomatoes to
    the list of ingredients)

About 1½ lb/675 g well-
    beaten mashed potatoes
    for the top of the pie

Heat the oil and cook the chopped onions till they are soft and turning golden brown. Add the chopped garlic, and stir in the flour (or the gravy, if you are using it). Cook for a minute, then stir in the tomato purée, water and lager, and stir till this sauce boils. Take the pan off the heat, stir in the salt, pepper and Worcestershire sauce. Cool the sauce completely before stirring in the pulverized leftover meat – I put mine into a food processor briefly. I don't like adding cooked meat to a hot sauce if it means a third reheating is going to be taking place later on – and as I always make a shepherd's pie well in advance, that is what would happen.

When the sauce is cold, stir in the meat, put this mixture into a heatproof dish and cover with the creamily beaten mashed potatoes. Fork into a neat pattern, and cook in a moderate oven, 350°F/180°C Gas Mark 4, for 35–40 minutes.

Beef (or Lamb) Cakes

I feel this is rather a clumsy name for a dish using up leftover roast beef or lamb which is similar in its make-up to a fish cake, in that the food-processed meat is combined with well-mashed potatoes flavoured with sautéed onions and garlic and seasoned, and the 'cakes' then fried in sunflower oil till they are crisp. They go very well with their extremely simple accompanying sauce consisting of Branston pickle mixed with whipped cream, or, if you feel this sauce doesn't appeal to you, then have a good tomato sauce (see page 156) instead.

SERVES 6

3 tbsp sunflower oil
2 onions, skinned and finely chopped
1–2 cloves of garlic, skinned and very finely chopped
About 1½ lb/675 g well-mashed potatoes, beaten with a wooden spoon with 2 tbsp Worcestershire sauce, 2 oz/56 g butter and 2 tbsp finely chopped parsley

About 1 lb/450 g leftover meat, weighed once trimmed of all gristle and fat; pulverize the meat in a food processor
2 eggs, beaten on a plate (I use a fork for this)
Plenty of fresh brown breadcrumbs
Oil for frying

Heat the oil and gently sauté the onions and garlic till the onions are beginning to turn golden brown. Cool, then mix with the cold very well beaten potatoes, and the pulverized meat. Shape into even-sized 'cakes' (like hamburgers) and dip them first in beaten egg, then in the breadcrumbs, on each side. Put them on a tray lined with greaseproof paper till you are ready to fry them.

In a preferably non-stick frying pan, heat a small amount of sunflower oil till very hot, and fry the meatcakes on each side for 3 or 4 minutes, till they are deep golden brown and very crisp. Keep warm on a dish lined with several thicknesses of absorbent kitchen paper, to absorb excess oil.

Devilled Tunafish

All the ingredients for this simple dish can be found – or rather, kept – in a storecupboard. I like to serve it with boiled Basmati rice and a green or mixed salad. If you have Kallo stock cubes in the storecupboard, these contain no additives, and one or two chicken cubes in the water in which you cook the rice makes a great difference and enhances the flavour. As an alternative, you can slice half a lemon and cook the rice with the lemon slices.

SERVES 6

2 oz/56 g butter	*1 clove of garlic, skinned*
2 oz/56 g flour	*and finely chopped*
1 pt/570 ml milk	*3 tbsp tomato ketchup*
Three 15–oz/420–g tins of	*(which must be Heinz)*
tunafish, well drained of	*4 tbsp breadcrumbs*
their oil or brine	*whizzed in a processor*
2 tbsp lemon juice	*with a good handful of*
2 tbsp dry sherry	*parsley, then both fried in*
2 tbsp Worcestershire	*2 tbsp sunflower oil and 1*
sauce	*oz/56 g butter till golden*
	and crisp

Melt the butter and stir in the flour. Cook for a minute before adding the milk, slowly, and stirring continuously till the sauce boils. Take the pan off the heat, stir in the drained tunafish, and the lemon juice, sherry, Worcestershire sauce, chopped garlic and tomato ketchup. Pour into a warmed serving dish, and scatter with the fried breadcrumbs and parsley.

Serve as soon as possible, although this will keep warm for up to 20 minutes without spoiling.

Pasta with Garlic, Olive Oil and Black Olives

Provided you have pasta in the storecupboard, and olive oil, olives and garlic, and some grated fresh Parmesan in the freezer, this is a real storecupboard supper which tastes delicious if you, like me, have distinctly Mediterranean tastes. The Parmesan will thaw during the time it takes for the water to boil to cook the pasta, and also during this time you can be chopping the garlic finely and stoning and cutting in half the olives. If you should happen to grow parsley, or have a bunch in the fridge, a few tablespoons of fairly coarsely chopped parsley adds even more taste, but if not, don't worry.

SERVES 6

About 1 lb/450 g pasta – I like spaghetti best for this, for no real reason except that it is my preference

As much extra virgin olive oil as you like, but at least ¼ pt/140 ml

2–3 cloves garlic, skinned and very finely chopped

As many black olives as you like, preferably the best, preserved in those distinctive red and gold cans with chopped herbs in with the olives; stone the olives, and cut in half or quarters

Finely chopped parsley if you have some

Lots of freshly ground black pepper

Boil the pasta in plenty of salted water till it is just tender but with a slight bite to it – al dente.

Drain the cooked pasta well, then put it back into the pan in which it was cooked and immediately stir in the olive oil, chopped garlic, chopped olives and parsley – if you are using it – and grind in lots of black pepper. Stir all together well, and eat immediately, with a bowl of freshly grated Parmesan cheese.

Curried Eggs

One of the dishes I remember from being a child and when staying with my grandmother was having curried eggs with boiled rice for supper. They make a good supper dish to this day, and can be put in the panic supper category provided you have one or two fresh items to hand as well – these are apples, onions and garlic. If you haven't had sultanas in a curry sauce before, and don't much like the sound of it, especially with eggs, please try it once – it really does make for a good curried sauce. You can make the curry as hot or not as you like by using medium or very hot curry powder.

SERVES 6

12 eggs	*2 tsp medium strength curry powder*
3 tbsp sunflower oil	*1 tbsp flour*
2 onions, skinned and finely chopped	*2 tbsp tomato purée*
1–2 cloves of garlic, skinned and very finely chopped	*2 tbsp lemon juice*
	1 pt/570 ml chicken stock (cube and water if in a panic!)
2 eating apples – ideally Cox's or similar in taste – peeled, cored and chopped	*3 oz/84 g sultanas*
	Boiled rice for six people

Hardboil the eggs – I boil them for 6 minutes and leave them to cool in their shells.

Heat the oil in a saucepan and cook the onions till they are just beginning to turn golden brown. Stir in the garlic, the apples and the curry powder. Stir in the flour and let all cook for a minute before mixing in the tomato purée, lemon juice and stock, stirring till the sauce boils. Add the sultanas, and let the sauce simmer very gently for 10 minutes, stirring from time to time to stop it sticking. Keep the sauce warm till you are ready to serve.

Shell the eggs and cut each one in half. Press them down into the rice and spoon the sauce over the top.

Stuffed Egg Salad

These eggs are stuffed with a sardine mixture which is loved even by those who profess to dislike sardines – and I really know this is so, because I am married to just such a one! The pâté takes the same time to make as the eggs take to hardboil, cool and shell.

Serve the stuffed eggs on a bed of shredded lettuce leaves, of whatever variety you can lay your hands on. The eggs are quite filling, but for a main course I allow two eggs, four halves, per person.

SERVES 6

Lettuce leaves, shredded
12 eggs
½ lb mushrooms, wiped,
  chopped, and sautéed in 2
  tbsp sunflower oil + 1 oz/
  28 g butter
Two 4½-oz/124-g tins of
  sardines in oil, well
  drained of their oil

Three 7-oz/200-g tubs of
  Philadelphia cream
  cheese, or their Lite
  alternative with reduced
  fat content
Juice of 1 lemon
Lots of freshly ground black
  pepper

Divide the shredded lettuce to cover six individual plates.

Hardboil the eggs by boiling for 7 minutes, then cooling under running water. Shell them, and carefully cut each in half, flicking out their yolks with the point of a knife into a bowl. Slice a very tiny piece off the base of each egg half, so that they will sit steadily on the plates, and put four halves on each plate.

Sauté the mushrooms in the oil-and-butter mixture over a high heat. Put the sardines, well drained, into a food processor with the Philadelphia cheese. Whiz, then add the mushrooms and whiz again, adding the lemon juice and black pepper. Whiz in the egg yolks. With a wide star-shaped nozzle, pipe this filling generously into the hole in each egg half, piling the filling up.

Arrange lettuce leaves around the eggs and have, if you like, a tomato salad to serve with them.

By the way, rinse out the piping bag thoroughly, then put it into your washing machine on your next boil load. I was given this tip, which makes washing piping bags so much easier.

Sautéed Chicken Livers with Onions, Apples and Cream

If you have a few cartons of chicken livers in your freezer, they can form the basis of an excellent panic supper. They really don't take very long to thaw, and they are much easier to pick over when semi-thawed, to remove the yellowy bits and any stringy bits. I allow two 8-oz/225-g cartons between three people. All you need for this dish is a couple of onions, a couple of apples, and a couple of cartons of long life single or double cream – and lots of Basmati rice to go with it.

SERVES 6

Four 8-oz/225-g cartons of
   chicken livers
2 tbsp sunflower oil + 1 oz/
   56 g butter
2 onions, skinned and finely
   chopped
1–2 cloves of garlic,
   skinned and very finely
   chopped
2 good eating apples, e.g.
   Cox's, or Granny Smith's
if you like a tarter
   flavour, peeled, cored and
   chopped
1 tsp medium strength
   curry powder
1 pt/570 ml single cream –
   you can use double if that
   is all you have
Salt and freshly ground
   black pepper

As soon as you can, tip the contents of the chicken liver cartons on to a plate or board, and chisel them apart – they will then thaw surprisingly quickly. When they are half-thawed, pick them over and remove any bits which don't appeal to you – any yellow bits, which mean they are bitter tasting. (The yellow was the bile!)

Heat the oil and melt the butter together in a frying pan or sauté pan, and cook the onions till they are just turning golden brown. Stir in the garlic and chopped apples. Cook, stirring from time to time, for about 5 minutes, then stir in the curry powder, the cream, the salt and lots of pepper. Let this bubble away gently while you heat the 2 tablespoons of oil in a separate sauté pan, and cook the livers till they just seize up, then transfer them to the pan with the sauce. Let all cook together for a few minutes before serving with boiled Basmati rice. Don't overcook the livers.

Cheese, Ham and Mushroom Puff Pastry Slice

Buying ready rolled out puff pastry is a great help for panic suppers, because it thaws reasonably quickly, and you can be making the filling while the pastry thaws. These are two long rectangular shapes, and you cut them in thick slices to serve them.

All you need is an accompanying salad – I think the pastry is quite filling enough not to make any other type of starch necessary.

SERVES 6

2 tbsp sunflower oil + 1 oz/56 g butter

2 onions, skinned and finely chopped

1 lb/450 g mushrooms, wiped and chopped

1–2 cloves of garlic, skinned and finely chopped

12 oz/340 g Cheddar cheese, grated

½ lb/225 g cooked ham (either boiled or roast), trimmed of fat and cut in cubes

½ teaspoon salt

Lots of freshly ground black pepper

2 eggs, beaten

1 packet of ready rolled out puff pastry, cut this into four even lengths, about 4 in/10 cm wide

1 egg, beaten (to brush the pastry before cooking)

Heat the oil and melt the butter together and cook the onions in this mixture till the onions turn golden brown. Scoop them on to a dish and raise the heat under the frying or sauté pan. Cook the mushrooms, stirring, till they almost squeak. Mix them in with the onions, and add the garlic, which will cook in the pastry. If you prefer a less pronounced garlic taste, cook it with the onions – the longer it cooks, the less the garlic is noticeable. Mix in the grated cheese, ham, salt, pepper and beaten eggs and spread this mixture on two of the four strips of pastry. Cover with the other strips and brush the tops with beaten egg.

Bake in a hot oven, 420°F/220°C/Gas Mark 7, till well puffed up and dark golden – about 20–25 minutes. Serve as soon as you can.

Tomato and Onion Tart

This is a variation on a quiche, with Parmesan-flavoured pastry and a filling of sautéed onions and skinned, de-seeded, chopped tomatoes. A combination of whole eggs and egg yolks with single cream makes the filling, which bakes till it is just set.

It needs a salad as an accompaniment.

SERVES 6

For the pastry:
3 oz/84 g butter, hard from the fridge, cut in bits
3 oz/84 g freshly grated Parmesan cheese
5 oz/140 g plain flour
A couple of pinches of salt
For the filling:
2 tbsp sunflower oil + 2 oz/ 56 g butter

4 onions, skinned and finely sliced
1–2 cloves of garlic, skinned and finely chopped
6 tomatoes
A few basil leaves, torn
2 whole eggs + 2 egg yolks beaten with ½ pt/285 ml single cream
Salt and freshly ground black pepper

Put all the ingredients for the pastry into a food processor and whiz till the mixture resembles fine crumbs. Pat this firmly around the sides and base of a flan dish measuring about 9 inches/23 cm in diameter.

Put the dish into the fridge for an hour, then bake in a moderate oven, 350°F/180°C/Gas Mark 4, till pale golden – about 20–25 minutes.

Make the filling by heating the oil and melting the butter, and cooking the onions in this, stirring from time to time. Cook them for 10 minutes, till they just begin to turn golden, then add the chopped garlic. Cook for a further few minutes. Spoon this over the baked pastry case.

Skin the tomatoes by stabbing them and then pouring boiling water over them for a few seconds. Drain away the water and the skins will slip off easily. Cut each tomato in half, scoop out the seeds, chop the tomato flesh and scatter it over the onions and garlic with the basil leaves. Season the eggs and cream mixture with salt and pepper and pour it over.

Bake till just set in a moderate oven, 350°F/180°C/Gas Mark 4 – about 25 minutes.

Mango and Curried Chicken Salad

Provided you have some cold chicken and three ripe mangoes, this salad takes seconds to make. It needs cold boiled Basmati rice to go with it, and a green salad. These are all ingredients which you can buy fairly easily, depending on where you live. I like to toss the cooked rice in a couple of spoonfuls of olive oil, with a little finely grated lemon rind and plenty of finely chopped parsley and snipped chives, all of which both make it look as well as taste much more interesting.

Serves 6

3 tsp medium curry powder	*A pinch of salt and plenty of freshly ground black pepper*
2 tbsp lemon juice	
2 tbsp runny honey	*6 cooked chicken breasts, or the meat from 1 whole cooked chicken*
6 tbsp good mayonnaise	
¼ pt/140 ml double cream, whipped	
	3 ripe mangoes, skin sliced off and flesh cut off the stone

Fold the curry powder, lemon juice and honey into the mayonnaise, then fold the whipped cream into this mixture and season it. Carefully fold the chicken and chopped mangoes into this sauce and arrange on a serving dish or plate. If you like, spoon the cooked lemon and herb rice around the edges.

Avocado and Bacon Salad with Pinhead Oatmeal Bread

You can, of course, serve this with any warm bread or rolls which you happen to have in the freezer, but this pinhead oatmeal and garlic bread is delicious, and altogether takes only about 45 minutes to make – you can freeze the extra loaves.

The salad is simplicity itself, and surprisingly filling. Although you can use back bacon, I much prefer to use streaky bacon for this, grilled till crisp.

SERVES 6

For the salad:
6 avocado pears
Lettuce leaves
Lemon juice
12 rashers smoked streaky bacon
Really good extra virgin olive oil
For the bread:
½ pt/285 ml hand-hot water with 1 tbsp sugar dissolved in it and 2 tbsp dried yeast, e.g.

Allinson's, stirred in well
2½ lb/1.125 kg wholemeal flour
½ lb/225 g pinhead oatmeal dry-toasted with 2 tsp salt
2 cloves of garlic, skinned and very finely chopped
1 pt/570 ml hot water with 2 tsp salt and 1 tbsp honey or molasses sugar stirred in

Pare off the skins of the avocado pears, flick out the stones, slice the flesh into slivers and arrange these fan-shaped on top of lettuce leaves on six individual plates. Brush them well with lemon juice to help prevent discolouring. Grill the bacon till crisp, then crumble it and divide it between the six plates. Pour olive oil over each.

To make the bread, leave the yeast liquid in a warm place till it forms a head of froth equal in size to the water beneath it. Then stir this into the flour, oatmeal and chopped garlic, and stir in the sugar-and-salt water. Mix well, then turn the dough on to a floured surface and knead – I knead to a count of 200. Divide the dough into three equal-sized bits, knead each one, and put them into three oiled tins. Cover with a teatowel and leave in a warm place till the dough has doubled in size in the tins.

Bake in a hot oven, 420°F/220°C/Gas Mark 7, for 15–20 minutes, till the loaves turn out of their tins and sound hollow when you tap them on the base. Cool on a wire rack, but not in a draught, which would toughen the cooling bread.

This bread is delicious toasted, as well as untoasted.

Tomato Cream Dressed Avocado Salad

This salad has the dressing as a vital part of the dish. You really do need to use a red-skinned, mild onion for this – if you can't, you can substitute finely sliced spring onions. The dressing can be made up ahead if you keep it in a covered bowl in the fridge.

SERVES 6

Assorted salad leaves	*¼ pt/140 ml good*
6 ripe avocados	*mayonnaise*
Lemon juice	*2 tsp red onion, very finely*
For the dressing:	*chopped*
8 tomatoes	*2 tbsp finely chopped*
¼ pt/140 ml creamy	*parsley*
fromage frais	*Salt and lots of freshly*
	ground black pepper

Arrange torn-up salad leaves on six individual plates. Peel the avocados and remove the stones. Slice each one thinly and arrange each one in a fan shape on top of the leaves. Brush the slices with lemon juice.

Put the tomatoes into a bowl and stab each one with the point of a knife. Pour over boiling water to cover them, and leave till you see the skins beginning to curl back from the stabbed places – several seconds. Drain the water off the tomatoes and skin them. Cut each in half, scoop away their seeds, and chop the flesh into fine dice. Fold these into the fromage frais together with the mayonnaise, finely chopped red onion, parsley, and salt and pepper to your taste.

Spoon the dressing over the avocados on their plates. This looks and tastes good.

Special Occasions

Watercress Roulade with Salmon and Fromage Frais

Stir-Fried Scallops with Ginger and Spring Onions

Cheese Profiteroles with Mushroom and Celery Filling

Leeks in Ham in Goats' Cheese Soufflé

Bacon, Tomato and Cheese Soufflé

Smoked Haddock (or Cod) Soufflé with Tomato Sauce

Mushroom, Garlic and Smoked Bacon Soufflé

Goulash with Beef, Red Peppers and Potatoes

Baked Chicken Breasts with Garlic, Onions and New Potatoes in Olive Oil

Baked Lamb Chops with Potatoes, Leeks and Cream

Pasta with Asparagus, Cream and Crispy Bacon Sauce

Smoked Haddock Timbales with Watercress Sauce

Crab Florentine with Sesame Toast

Stir-Fried Chicken with Ginger, Cardamom and Cashew Nuts

Chicken with Aubergines, Tomatoes and Garlic

Turkey Fillets with Onions, Mushrooms and Fromage Frais

Roast Lamb with Anchovies

Barbecued Sea Bass with Soya Sauce

Squid with Garlic and Parsley in Olive Oil

Pheasant Breasts with Creamy Bacon Sauce

Calves' Liver with Mousseline Potatoes, Sautéed Baby Onions and Spinach
with Fried Pinenuts

Baked Ham Slices in Tomato and White Wine Sauce

Creamy Mushroom, Garlic and Bacon Sauce for Pasta

Peanut Chicken

Peppered Steak with Stilton and Chive Butter

*Stir-Fried Monkfish with Jerusalem Artichokes,
Ginger and Garlic*

SPECIAL OCCASIONS

The recipes in this chapter cover a multitude of occasions when a straightforward supper becomes, if not an out-and-out dinner party, rather more special a meal than an everyday supper. Events which qualify for this special treatment are birthdays and anniversaries, St Valentine's Day, last suppers at home before the beginning of school or university terms, and just as important and with an added atmosphere of joy missing from the last, the first supper on homecoming, whether from school, university, or wherever.

When we were children and living in Rome, luckily there was one thing on which we all three sisters were agreed, and that was our choice of last and first suppers of the holidays. They never varied, and consisted of calves' liver, fried tiny onions, very well mashed potatoes, and puréed spinach with fried pinenuts.

Special occasion food does not mean elaborate dishes. Far from it – many of the dishes in this chapter are meal-in-one dishes. For example, the Baked Chicken Breasts with Garlic, Onions and New Potatoes in Olive Oil, or any of the soufflés, the Stir-Fried Chicken with Ginger, Cardamon and Cashew Nuts, or the very simple but delicious Pasta with Asparagus, Cream and Crispy Bacon Sauce. All of these need only an accompanying salad as well as, perhaps in the case of the stir-fry, boiled rice. A special occasion meal certainly doesn't need to consist of a first course, meat and two veg, and a pudding, it just needs to be favourite food which in so many cases can be prepared, if not actually cooked, well in advance.

In this chapter are recipes for dishes using meat, fish and chicken and turkey, usually combined with simple but good vegetable and spice ingredients, to give a more special feeling to the meal overall.

Watercress Roulade with Salmon and Fromage Frais

This makes an elegant main course for a special occasion. It is convenient in that it can be made in stages, i.e. the roulade can be made the previous day, and filled and rolled up several hours before being served. It also makes ideal smart picnic food, when a rather more up-market picnic is called for on occasions like a parents' day at school. Provided it is packed into a cold box, it travels beautifully. It has the benefit of both looking and tasting good, because the watercress keeps its bright colour after cooking, as well as its distinctive slightly peppery flavour.

SERVES 6–8

For the flavoured milk:
1 pt/570 ml milk
1 skinned onion, cut in half
1 stick of celery, broken in two
A few crushed parsley stalks (crushing them releases their flavour)
½ teaspoon rock salt
A good grinding of black pepper
A 3-oz/84 g bag of watercress

For the roulade:
2 oz/56 g butter
2 oz/56 g flour
The flavoured milk
A grating of nutmeg
4 large eggs, separated
For the filling:
½ pt/285 ml creamy fromage frais
8–10 oz/225–285 g cooked salmon, flaked, skin and bones removed
2 tbsp finely chopped parsley and snipped chives, mixed

Heat the milk in a saucepan with the onion, celery, parsley stalks, salt and pepper till a skin forms. Take the saucepan off the heat and leave for an hour. Strain the milk into a jug and throw away the flavourings. Liquidize this milk with the well-washed watercress.

Line a baking tray with a sheet of siliconized greaseproof paper. Make the roulade by melting the butter in a saucepan and stir in the flour. Cook this for a minute, then stir in the flavoured milk and liquidized watercress, stirring the sauce continuously till it boils. Season with a grating of nutmeg, taste, and add more salt and pepper if you think it needs it. Beat in the yolks, one by one. In a scrupulously clean bowl whisk the whites till they are stiff and, with a large metal spoon, fold them quickly and thoroughly through the watercress sauce. Pour this into the lined tin and bake in a moderately hot oven, 350°F/180°C/Gas Mark 4, for 30–35 minutes. The top should be puffed up and golden brown and it should feel firm. Take it out of the oven and cover with a damp teatowel. Leave to cool completely.

To turn out and complete the roulade, lay a fresh sheet of siliconized greaseproof paper on a table or work surface. Holding the short ends of the paper under the cooked roulade in either hand, flip it over, face down, on to the fresh paper. Peel off the paper from the back of the roulade, tearing it in strips parallel with the surface. Spread the fromage frais over the surface, right up to the edges. Fork the flaked salmon evenly over the fromage frais. Scatter the snipped chives and chopped parsley over all. Roll it up away from you, and slip it on to a serving plate.

If you intend taking the roulade on a picnic, cover the dish with clingfilm.

Stir-Fried Scallops with Ginger and Spring Onions

This is such a quick dish to cook. As with all fish and shellfish, scallops are ruined by overcooking, and once sliced, they need the briefest cooking in the hot butter and oil with the ginger and spring onions. And don't worry about the ginger and spring onions if you haven't tried this combination before, believe me, it really is delicious. Ginger when fresh in unbelievably fiery, but as soon as it starts to cook it loses its ferocity. With 2 or 3 minutes cooking before you add the scallops, the hot ginger will have subsided to a gentle glow of flavour. The spring onions are good not just in taste, but also in appearance, because as they cook they intensify in colour.

This needs as accompaniment boiled Basmati rice (by far the best-tasting rice) and a green salad.

SERVES 6

18 scallops – 3 each is plenty if they are medium-sized scallops	*2 oz/56 g butter + 2 tbsp sunflower oil*
2 bunches of spring onions	*¼ pt/140 ml single cream*
About 2-in/5-cm piece of fresh ginger	*Salt and freshly ground black pepper*

Slice each scallop in three widthwise. Trim the spring onions of outer leaves, and chop off the ends. Slice each spring onion in diagonal slices about ¼ inch/½cm wide. Peel off the skin from the ginger and chop it finely.

Heat the butter and oil together in a wide pan and cook the onions and ginger together for 2–3 minutes, stirring continuously. Then add the sliced scallops and cook for a further minute or two till they turn opaque. Stir in the cream, salt and pepper, and bubble for 1 minute.

Pour into a warmed serving dish and keep warm till you are ready to dish up and serve.

Cheese Profiteroles with Mushroom and Celery Filling

These are convenient in that the large cheese choux buns can be made well in advance – two or three days ahead – and stored in an airtight container, or frozen. If they are frozen, give them a couple of hours to thaw at room temperature, and reheat them in a moderate oven for 5 minutes whether they have been made a day or more in advance, frozen or not. This will refresh the flavour as well as the texture. The filling can be made in the morning for dinner that night, and then just spooned into the profiteroles before they are heated, about half an hour before supper-time.

Because of the choux pastry, I think it best to skip other starch and opt instead for two vegetables as accompaniment, for example, a purée of root vegetables like carrot and parsnip with fried cashew nuts as a crunchy garnish, and perhaps broccoli, steamed till just tender in the stalk, and then with good olive oil poured over and let cool, to serve at room temperature. The broccoli absorbs the flavour of the olive oil as it cools.

SERVES 6

For the cheese profiteroles:
5 oz/140 g butter, cut in bits
½ pt/285 ml water
6 oz/170 g plain flour
1 heaped tsp mustard powder
3 oz/84 g grated cheese – a good strong Cheddar
1 clove of garlic, skinned and finely chopped
A dash of Worcestershire sauce
4 large eggs

For the filling:
3 oz/84 g butter + 1 tbsp sunflower oil
½ lb/225 g mushrooms, wiped and chopped quite small
1 clove of garlic, skinned and finely chopped
3 sticks of celery, trimmed and sliced very finely
2 level tbsp flour
1 pt/570 ml milk
Salt and plenty of freshly ground black pepper
A grinding of nutmeg
2 oz/56 g Cheddar cheese, grated

In a saucepan melt the butter in the water, taking great care not to let the liquid boil until the butter is completely melted. Sieve the flour and mustard powder twice, and as soon as the butter-water comes to the boil, add the flour all in one go and beat like mad till the mixture comes away from the sides of the pan – this will only take about half a minute. Take the pan off the heat and beat in the grated cheese, finely chopped garlic and Worcestershire sauce. Beat in the eggs, one by one, beating really well in between each.

Rinse a baking sheet with cold water. With a piping bag and a wide star-shaped nozzle pipe the choux pastry in mounds about the size of a ping-pong ball.

Bake in a hot oven, 400°F/200°C/Gas Mark 6, for 25–30 minutes, checking them after 20 minutes and turning the tray around if necessary. The profiteroles should be puffed up, golden brown and feel firm when cooked. Cut a slit in the side of each 5 minutes before their cooking time is up – this lets the steam within each escape.

To make the filling, melt the butter and heat the oil together in a saucepan. When it is very hot add the chopped mushrooms, finely chopped garlic and sliced celery and cook over a high heat, stirring, till the mushrooms are almost crisp – cooking them to this extent improves their flavour. Lower the heat a bit and continue cooking the mushrooms and celery and garlic for a further 2 or 3 minutes, then stir in the flour. Cook this mixture for a minute before gradually adding the milk, stirring continuously till the sauce boils.

Take the pan off the heat and stir in the salt, pepper, nutmeg and grated cheese. If you are making the sauce in advance, at this point press down over the surface of the sauce a piece of greaseproof paper wrung out in water; this prevents a skin forming on the top of the sauce.

Before serving, cut each profiterole in half and spoon in the filling, dividing it between the profiteroles. Put the halves together, place them in an ovenproof dish and reheat them in a moderately hot oven, 350°F/180°C/Gas Mark 4, for 15 minutes.

Leeks in Ham in Goats' Cheese Soufflé

This is a substantial dish, and needs no further accompaniment other than, perhaps, a green or a mixed salad, and warm bread or rolls. For anyone who hasn't had cooked goats' cheese before, the taste is delicious, and it is particularly complemented by leeks.

Soufflés do not mean last-minute cooking with the whites needing to be whisked and folded in just before the soufflé is cooked. Several years ago I was taught by my great friend Char Hunt that a soufflé is every bit as successful if the whites are whisked and folded into the rest of the soufflé mixture and poured into the prepared dish, in this case on top of the ham and leeks, the dish covered with clingfilm and left for two or three hours before the soufflé is cooked. (Don't forget to whip off the clingfilm before putting the dish into the oven, though.)

SERVES 6

12 medium leeks, trimmed, well washed, and steamed till just tender	2 oz/56 g self-raising flour
	3/4 pt/420 ml milk
	Salt and lots of freshly ground black pepper
12 very thin slices of ham	A grating of nutmeg
For the soufflé:	8 oz/225 g goats' cheese
2 oz/56 g butter	4 large eggs, separated

Butter an oval or oblong ovenproof dish. Wrap each just-cooked leek in a slice of the wafer-thin ham and arrange these in the buttered dish. Make the soufflé by melting the butter in a saucepan and stirring in the flour. Let it cook for a minute before pouring in the milk gradually, stirring continuously till the sauce boils.

Take the pan off the heat and season with salt, pepper and the nutmeg, and stir in the goats' cheese. Beat in the yolks, one by one, and lastly whisk the whites till they are very stiff. With a large metal spoon, fold the whisked whites quickly and thoroughly through the cheese sauce. Pour this over the ham-wrapped leeks.

Bake in a hot oven, 425°F/220°C/Gas Mark 7, for 30 minutes – the soufflé should be very slightly runny in the middle.

If you want to prepare the soufflé ahead, when you have folded in the whites, cover the dish with clingfilm and leave it in a cool place till you are ready to bake it. Remove the clingfilm and cook it as described. Once cooked, it must be eaten immediately. There can be no sadder sight than that of a slowly but inexorably sinking soufflé!

Bacon, Tomato and Cheese Soufflé

I always think that bits, or to put it more elegantly texture, in a soufflé makes it far more interesting to eat. This soufflé has chopped tomatoes which are skinned and de-seeded (to prevent them being too watery) and diced lean smoked bacon to add interest in texture as well as taste. If you can get good Lancashire cheese the soufflé will be the better for it, but if not, use Cheddar cheese.

Soufflés are more filling than one imagines them to be, and this needs just a salad and warm bread or rolls to go with it.

SERVES 6

2 tbsp fresh Parmesan cheese, grated	3 oz/84 g self-raising flour
3 oz/84 g butter	1¼ pts/710 ml milk
6 rashers of smoked back bacon, trimmed of most of its fat and diced quite finely	8 oz/225 g Lancashire cheese, crumbled
1 large clove of garlic, skinned and very finely chopped (if you don't love garlic as I do, you can leave this out)	Salt and freshly ground black pepper
	A grating of nutmeg
	8 large eggs, separated
	6 tomatoes, each skinned, cut in half and seeds removed, then cut in neat strips or chopped

Butter two same-sized soufflé dishes or similar ovenproof dishes, and dust them out with grated Parmesan cheese.

Melt the butter in a saucepan and add the diced bacon and the finely chopped garlic. Cook, stirring, for several minutes till the bacon is cooked through. Stir in the flour, then gradually add the milk, stirring continuously till the sauce boils.

Take the pan off the heat and stir in the crumbled cheese, the salt, pepper and nutmeg. Beat in the yolks, one by one. Whisk the whites till they are very stiff and, with a large metal spoon, fold them and the chopped tomatoes quickly and thoroughly through the sauce.

Divide the soufflé mixture between the two prepared dishes and either cover them with clingfilm and bake later, or bake them straight away, in a hot oven, 425°F/220°C/Gas Mark 7, for 30–35 minutes. Serve immediately.

Smoked Haddock (or Cod) Soufflé with Tomato Sauce

Thank heavens that we can all get good smoked haddock these days without having to search too hard for it. It isn't very many years since smoked haddock meant brilliant yellow, rubbery little fillets, whereas what I want – and can now get with comparative ease – is large, juicy, undyed, pale-coloured smoked fish. And I love smoked cod, too, as much as smoked haddock.

This soufflé is a favourite with our family who luckily all love fish. The soufflé is made using the milk in which the fish cooked briefly before being flaked. Serving a sauce with a soufflé can be looked upon as both a garnish and an integral part of the whole.

SERVES 6

2 lb/900 g smoked haddock or cod	1¼ pts/710 ml of the fish milk
1 onion, skinned and cut in half	Plenty of freshly ground black pepper (the fish will be sufficiently salty for most palates)
2 pts/1.1 L milk	
3 oz/84 g butter	
3 oz/84 g self-raising flour	8 large eggs, separated

For the tomato sauce:
3 tbsp olive oil
1 onion, skinned and finely
  chopped
2 sticks of celery,
  trimmed and very finely
  sliced

1 clove of garlic, skinned
  and very finely chopped
Two 15-oz/420-g tins
  chopped tomatoes,
  drained of excess juice
Salt and freshly ground
  black pepper
½ teaspoon sugar

Put the fish into a saucepan with the halved onion and the milk. Over a moderate heat cook till a skin forms on the milk, then take the pan off the heat, and leave the fish to cool in the milk. Strain 1¼ pints/710 ml of the milk into a jug. Flake the fish, throwing away all bones and skin, into a bowl.

Butter two soufflé dishes, or same-sized ovenproof dishes. Melt the 3 ounces/84 g of butter in a saucepan and stir in the flour. Let it cook for a minute, then stir in the reserved fish milk, stirring till the sauce boils.

Take the pan off the heat, season with pepper and beat in the egg yolks one by one. Whisk the whites till they are very stiff and, with a large metal spoon, fold them and the flaked cooked fish through the sauce.

Divide this soufflé mixture between the two buttered dishes and bake in a hot oven, 425°F/220°C/Gas Mark 7, for 30 minutes. Serve immediately they are cooked – they should be slightly runny in the middle.

To make the tomato sauce, heat the oil in a saucepan and add the chopped onion, sliced celery and finely chopped garlic. Cook, stirring occasionally, till the onion is soft and transparent-looking, about 5 minutes. Stir in the drained, chopped tomatoes, season with salt, pepper and sugar, and simmer the sauce gently for 15–20 minutes. You can either liquidize this sauce and serve it smooth or, provided you have chopped the onion and celery finely enough, you can serve it with its very slightly chunky texture. Whichever way, the sauce can be made in advance and reheated to serve. It also freezes well.

Mushroom, Garlic .
and Smoked Bacon Soufflé

This is another convenient but delicious soufflé with very complementary flavours and a good and interesting texture. I love garlic
bread with this, and a salad. I was taught, by a great friend (one of
the very best cooks I know, Brigadier Ley), that by cooking
mushrooms till they almost squeak, their flavour is vastly improved
in comparison to mushrooms which are just lightly sautéed.

SERVES 6

3 oz/84 g butter + 2 tbsp sunflower oil (the mushrooms use up quite a lot of butter during their cooking)	*1 lb/450 g mushrooms, wiped and neatly chopped*
1 onion, skinned and very finely chopped	*1 large clove of garlic, skinned and finely chopped*
6 rashers of smoked back bacon, fat trimmed off and the rashers diced quite small	*3 oz/84 g self-raising flour*
	1¼ pts/710 ml milk
	Salt and freshly ground black pepper
	A grating of nutmeg
	8 large eggs, separated

Butter two even-sized soufflé dishes, or 2 same-sized ovenproof
(pyrex, for example) dishes. Melt the butter and heat the oil
together in a saucepan and add the chopped onion and the diced
bacon. Cook till the onion is transparent – about 5 minutes over a
moderate heat. Then scoop this mixture on to a warmed plate,
keeping as much butter and oil in the pan as you can. Raise the heat
and when it is very hot, add the chopped mushrooms. Cook,
stirring, till they are almost crisp. Then take the pan off the heat
and turn it back down to moderate.

Replace the onion and bacon mixture in the pan and add the

chopped garlic (which, if it cooks for too long, won't make its presence felt in the cooked soufflé). Stir in the flour, cook for a minute, then gradually add the milk, stirring continuously till the sauce boils.

Take the pan off the heat, season with the salt, pepper and nutmeg, and beat in the egg yolks, one by one. Whisk the whites till they are very stiff and, with a large metal spoon, fold them quickly and thoroughly through the mushroom sauce.

Divide the soufflé mixture evenly between the two buttered dishes and either cover each dish with clingfilm, ready to cook several hours later, or cook straight away in a hot oven, 425°F/220°C/Gas Mark 7, for 30 minutes. Serve immediately.

Goulash with
Beef, Red Peppers and Potatoes

One of my favourite ways of cooking potatoes is to sauté them in butter and oil with sliced onions and paprika. This dish just combines the potatoes with the meat. It is a variation on a proper goulash, and a lot depends on the paprika, the quality of which varies considerably. If you can get good paprika do try it, it is a world apart from the average little tubs of paprika to be found on supermarket shelves. It is worthwhile skinning the peppers, too, even if it does sound rather a fiddle. The end result is so much nicer. And the whole dish is better made in advance, so it is convenient anyway.

This is good served with steamed cabbage, or just with a green salad.

SERVES 6

3–4 tbsp sunflower oil
2½ lbs/1.25 kg braising beef,
cut into 1–in/2.5–cm
pieces, and trimmed of
fat and any gristle
3 red peppers
3 onions, skinned and very
thinly sliced
2 cloves of garlic, skinned
and finely chopped

3 tbsp paprika
Salt and freshly ground
black pepper
12 medium potatoes, peeled
and boiled till they are
not quite cooked, then
well drained and cut in
chunks about the same
size as the beef

Heat the oil in a heavy casserole. Brown the beef, a little at a time, removing it as it browns to a warm dish. Meanwhile, under a hot grill, toast the peppers, each cut in half, skin side uppermost, till the skins are bubbling and charring. When they reach this stage put them in a polythene bag and leave them for 10 minutes. Then their skins will peel off easily. Chop them.

Once the meat is all browned, add the sliced onions to the casserole and cook them, stirring occasionally, till they are soft and beginning to turn golden. Then scoop them out of the casserole and in with the meat, and put the chopped peppers and garlic into the casserole. Cook for 3 to 5 minutes, stirring occasionally. Replace the meat and onions in the casserole, and stir in the paprika, salt and pepper. Carefully stir in the chopped parboiled potatoes, and cover the casserole with its lid.

Cook in a moderate oven, 350°F/180°C/Gas Mark 4, for 1 hour. Take the casserole out of the oven, let it cool, then store it in the fridge or a cold larder. To reheat to serve, bring the casserole into room temperature for an hour before putting it into a moderate oven for a further 35–40 minutes' cooking. If you like, stir ¼ pint/140 ml Greek or creamy natural yoghurt through the goulash just before serving – this is optional.

Baked Chicken Breasts with Garlic, Onions and New Potatoes in Olive Oil

This is one of the dishes most chosen by our children throughout the year when I give them the chance! It couldn't be simpler, but you have to beware not to overcook the chicken breasts. There is no need to overcook them, providing you sautée the sliced onions first in the olive oil. The small new potatoes take the same amount of time to cook as do the chicken breasts. Another point is to use the chicken breasts with skin on, not the skinless ones which would dry up horribly. Adjust the quantity of garlic cloves you include to suit your tastes. We love it!

SERVES 6

4 tbsp olive oil

3 onions, skinned and finely sliced

1½ lb/675 g tiny new potatoes, scrubbed

6 chicken breasts, with skin

6–12 cloves of garlic, each skinned and left whole

Salt and freshly ground black pepper

¼ pt/140 ml olive oil

Heat the 4 tbsp olive oil in a heavy, shallow casserole or sauté pan. Add the sliced onions and cook till they are just turning colour. Put the new potatoes in with the onions, turning them over so they get coated in oil, and put the chicken breasts on top of the potatoes. Scatter the skinned garlic cloves around the chicken. Season with salt and pepper and pour the olive oil over the lot in a thin trickle.

Cook, uncovered, in a hot oven, 400°F/200°C/Gas Mark 6, for about 30–35 minutes, till when you stick a fork in a potato it feels tender. Stab a chicken joint with the point of a sharp knife – any juices should run clear. This dish keeps warm in a cool oven satisfactorily for about 15–20 minutes.

Baked Lamb Chops with Potatoes, Leeks and Cream

Leeks and potatoes cooked together complement each other extremely well (think of vichysoisse) and the sweetness of the leeks enhances the flavour of the lamb in this all-in-one dish. The very small amount of medium curry powder won't be noticed by any partaker who thinks they don't like curry, I promise you, but it does just round off the overall flavour well.

SERVES 6

6 large, double lamb chops	1 tsp medium strength curry powder
6–8 medium to large leeks	½ pt/285 ml single cream
8 medium potatoes	Salt and freshly ground black pepper
2 oz/56 g butter + 2 tbsp sunflower oil	

Trim excess fat from the lamb chops. Wash and trim the leeks, and slice them diagonally into slices about 1 inch/2.5 cm thick. Peel the potatoes and slice them thinly. In a wide shallow pan – a sauté pan or a deep frying pan – melt the butter and heat the oil together. Brown the chops on each side, removing them to a large ovenproof dish as they are browned. Sauté the sliced leeks with the curry powder, stirring occasionally, for about 3–5 minutes. Take the pan off the heat.

Lift up the chops and arrange a layer of sliced potatoes to a depth of about ½ inch/1½ cm under the chops. Put the sautéed leeks over the chops, and cover with the remaining sliced potatoes. Pour in the cream and season with salt and pepper.

Bake uncovered in a moderate oven, 350°F/180°C/Gas Mark 4, for 25 minutes, then cover the dish and continue to cook for a further 20 minutes.

Pasta with Asparagus, Cream and Crispy Bacon Sauce

This is one of those special occasion dishes which take about 5 minutes to assemble and 5 to put together. If you are making it for non-meat-eaters you obviously won't want to include the bacon, so I suggest chopped cashew nuts which have been fried in a small amount of butter with a pinch or two of salt. This gives a good contrasting crunchy texture, as well as a complementary taste.

Which pasta you use depends on you. I like to make this dish using short pasta, that is, not spaghetti or tagliatelle, but shell shapes or bows. You only need a salad to go with it.

SERVES 6

1 lb/450 g asparagus	*A grating of nutmeg*
About 18 oz/500 g pasta, preferably bow or shell shapes	*6 rashers of smoked streaky bacon, grilled till crisp, then broken into small bits*
³/₄ pt/420 ml single cream	
Freshly ground black pepper (the bacon should add enough saltiness)	*1–2 tbsp chopped parsley and snipped chives, mixed*

Apart from the pasta, the other ingredients can be cooked or prepared in advance, so all you need to do before supper is cook the pasta and add the ready prepared ingredients. Prepare the asparagus by chopping off and throwing away the tough ends, and cutting it into pieces about 1 inch/2.5 cm long. Steam the pieces until just tender, but don't undercook it – I think that undercooked asparagus has a rather revolting taste.

Cook the pasta in plenty of boiling salted water or, better still, in vegetable or chicken stock. When it is just tender (stick a clean thumbnail into a piece to test it), drain it, return it to the pan, and add the steamed asparagus, single cream, pepper and nutmeg. Just before serving, stir in the chopped bacon, parsley and chives.

Serve immediately! If you like, have a bowl of freshly grated Parmesan to hand around.

Smoked Haddock Timbales with Watercress Sauce

These make a most delicious as well as convenient supper. You can make up the smoked haddock mixture in the morning ready to bake in the evening, but keep it in a jug and stir it up well with either a fork or a flat wire whisk before pouring it into the oiled ramekins. They take exactly half an hour to bake in a moderate oven, and they are no problem at all to turn out. They look so pretty surrounded by watercress sauce, and the taste of the sauce, too, is very complementary to that of the smoked fish.

With this main course, I feel a need for a crunchy vegetable, and my favourite with just about everything is sugar snap peas, each pea sliced diagonally into about three bits, and stir-fried with finely chopped garlic and fresh ginger which has already been given a head start in the frying pan of about 3 minutes before the peas are added – the peas need the briefest cooking time, about 30 seconds.

SERVES 6

2 lb/400 g smoked haddock	For the watercress sauce:
1¹/₂–2 pts/850–1100 ml milk and water mixed	*A 3-oz/84-g bag of watercress*
8 large eggs	*¹/₂ pt/285 ml milk*
³/₄ pt/420 ml single cream	*2 oz/56 g butter*
Plenty of freshly ground black pepper	*¹/₂ tsp cornflour*
A grating of nutmeg	*1 whole egg + 2 yolks*
	Salt and pepper
	A grating of nutmeg

Feel down the centre of each fillet of fish and carefully cut away the bones. Cut the fish into bits about 1 inch/2.5 cm in size and put them into a saucepan with the milk and water mixture. Bring the liquid around the fish to the point where a skin forms on the surface, then drain the fishy liquid away (keep it for soup) and put the partially cooked pieces of fish into a food processor. Whiz, gradually adding the eggs and cream. Season with pepper and a small amount of freshly grated nutmeg.

Oil twelve large ramekins and pour in the mixture. Carefully put each ramekin into a large baking tray deep enough for you to pour water in around the ramekins. Bake in a moderate oven, 350°F/180°C/Gas Mark 4, for 30 minutes.

Put the ingredients for the sauce into a liquidizer and whiz till smooth. If you have a microwave oven, put the sauce into a pyrex bowl on a medium heat for 2 minutes. Whisk well, then repeat the cooking process. Do this a third time, and the sauce should be thickened. If you don't have a microwave oven, put the bowl over a pan of simmering water, with the water coming up the sides of the bowl. Stir it with a whisk from time to time as it cooks – it will take 20–25 minutes, depending on the depth of the water around the bowl.

Turn out the timbales by running a knife around the inside of each ramekin and turning out two on each serving plate. Pour the sauce around the timbales, and serve. They will sit without deteriorating too much for 10 minutes or so – much longer than that and they seem to lose their initial airy texture.

Crab Florentine with Sesame Toast

I love crab. In this dish the flaked crabmeat, a mixture of white and brown meat, is on a bed of steamed spinach with a faint seasoning of nutmeg – a spice which enhances the taste of both the crab and the spinach – with cheese on top. The cheese sauce is set with the addition of egg, so that the whole thing isn't too runny.

The recipe for Sesame Toast is on page 89. It can be made in advance and reheated to serve. Store it in an airtight container.

SERVES 6

3 *lb/1.35 kg fresh spinach* *– this seems an awful* *lot, I realize, but I* *reckon on 1 lb/450 g* *fresh for two servings;* *once it is steamed, it* *diminishes by about* *four-fifths* *Grated nutmeg* *Salt and freshly ground* *black pepper* *1 lb/450 g crabmeat, white* *and brown mixed*	For the cheese sauce: *2 oz/56 g butter* *2 oz/56 g flour* *1 pt/570 ml milk* *4 oz/112 g grated Cheddar* *cheese – keep about ⅓* *aside for the surface* *Salt and freshly ground* *black pepper* *1 whole egg + 2 large egg* *yolks, beaten together*

Butter an ovenproof dish. Steam the spinach till it wilts, then, in a bowl, chop it with a very sharp knife, and mix in a grating of nutmeg, a pinch of salt and some black pepper. Chop it as finely as you can – but don't be tempted to purée it, because I personally like the texture of the chopped spinach with the flaked crab – otherwise, the whole dish tends to be rather mushy eating. Put it into the dish and distribute the crab over it.

Make the cheese sauce by melting the butter in a saucepan and stirring in the flour. Let it cook for a minute or two, then gradually add the milk, stirring all the time till the sauce boils. Take the pan off the heat and stir in two-thirds of the grated cheese, season with salt and pepper, and beat in the egg and egg yolks mixture. Pour this over the crab and sprinkle the remaining cheese over the surface.

Bake in a moderate oven, 180°F/200°C/Gas Mark 4, till the cheese sauce is just set – about 20–25 minutes. Serve with Sesame Toast.

Stir-Fried Chicken with Ginger, Cardamom and Cashew Nuts

Our family unanimously love stir-fried food. In Godfrey's case, it is partly because he loves any dish which has rice served as an accompaniment – he would eat rice and something every single day given the chance. But he, along with me and our four children, loves food which is cooked at a high temperature very briefly, which is what stir-frying is. It is really convenience cooking, in that the actual cooking takes such a very little time. The preparation, however, even though it can be done several hours ahead, does take a little time, because it is necessary to slice and chop the ingredients very finely. But even this needn't take very long provided you have a really sharp knife.

SERVES 6

8 chicken breasts (for growing offspring, 1 chicken breast per person isn't quite enough), each breast sliced into as thin matchsticks as possible

About 18 spring onions, each trimmed and sliced into thin sticks

4 cardamom seeds, crushed (with the end of a rolling pin or in a pestle and mortar)

2 in/5 cm fresh root ginger, pared of its skin and finely chopped

1–2 cloves of garlic (depending on your taste), peeled and finely chopped

3 tsp cornflour

3 tbsp strong soya sauce

2 tbsp dry sherry

½ pt/285 ml chicken stock

3 tbsp sunflower oil

3 oz/84 g cashew nuts, chopped and fried in butter and salt till golden brown – or bought already salted, then chopped

Put the strips of chicken, sliced spring onions, crushed cardamom, chopped ginger and garlic in a bowl, and mix together well. Mix together the conrflour, soya sauce, sherry and stock. Leave for several hours.

Heat the oil in a large, deep frying or sauté pan, add the chicken, spring onions, ginger and garlic mixture, and stir-fry in the very hot oil till the strips of chicken turn opaque. Then pour in the cornflour and liquids – stirring this mixture up well before you add it because the cornflour tends to sink to the bottom. Stir till the sauce boils, then dish up the contents of the pan (or wok) into a warmed serving dish, and scatter the chopped cashew nuts over the surface.

Serve with boiled Basmati rice, and a salad – I think a green salad containing chopped oranges and snipped chives seems to go very well with this stir-fry.

Chicken with Aubergines, Tomatoes and Garlic

This dish combines truly Mediterranean tastes with chicken. It can be made in advance and reheated – in fact, I think it is better made ahead. It really is necessary to cut up the aubergine and leave them to sit for half an hour before cooking them – the juices which seep out of them are bitter and indigestible, and the aubergines are so much nicer given this treatment. As they cook they collapse and their pulp gives a substance as well as a delicious flavour to the tomatoes, garlic and chicken in the olive oil.

This is good served with either steamed new potatoes or baked jacket potatoes, and a salad.

2 medium aubergines – 3 if they are small	2–3 cloves of garlic, each skinned and finely chopped
6 chicken breasts, with their skin on	8 tomatoes, skinned, cut in wedges and the seeds removed
2 tbsp flour sieved with ½ tsp salt and black pepper	
4 tbsp olive oil – extra virgin, preferably	

Slice the aubergines in half lengthways and cut them into chunks, about 1 inch/2.5 cm in size. Put them in a wide shallow bowl and sprinkle them with a little salt. Leave them for 30 minutes, then drain off the liquid which will have seeped out of them, and pat the chunks of aubergine dry with absorbent kitchen paper. Meanwhile, press each chicken breast in the seasoned flour.

Heat the oil in a wide saucepan – a deep frying pan or a sauté pan ideally – and brown the chicken on each side. Remove the chicken to a warmed dish. Add the chunks of aubergine to the oil in the pan – add more oil if necessary, and cook over a moderate heat, stirring occasionally, till the aubergine is beginning to brown, about 10 minutes. Stir in the chopped garlic and the tomatoes, and push the pieces of chicken down amongst the other ingredients.

If the pan has a lid, cover it and bake in a moderate oven, 350°F/ 180°C/Gas Mark 4, for 30 minutes if you intend to serve it straight away, or for 20 minutes if you intend to cool it, and re-cook it at a later date. Re-cook it by taking the dish into room temperature an hour before cooking, and cooking it in a moderate oven till the juices bubble, then let them bubble for 10 minutes.

If you have some, just before serving stir some basil leaves, torn rather than chopped with a knife (which turns the leaves brown), through the chickeny stew.

Turkey Fillets with Onions, Mushrooms and Fromage Frais

My second daughter, Isabella, asked me to include this recipe because she thought it was so delicious. But I didn't make it up, a great friend of ours, Caroline Gordon-Duff, made it while on holiday in Corsica, when Isabella was staying with them. Turkey fillets can be bought easily in most supermarkets and butchers' shops. They are usually skinless, and don't need very much cooking. If for any reason you can't get turkey fillets, just substitute skinless chicken fillets.

SERVES 6

3 oz/84 g butter + 2 tbsp sunflower oil
2 pieces of turkey fillet per person – or 1 if they are large (sometimes the fillets are packaged split)
2 onions, skinned and very thinly sliced
1–2 cloves of garlic, skinned and very finely chopped

³/₄ lb/340 g mushrooms, wiped and sliced
1 pt/570 ml fromage frais, if possible not the low fat type, the creamy fromage frais
Salt and freshly ground black pepper

Have ready a warmed ovenproof dish. Melt the butter and heat the oil together in a wide pan – a deep frying pan or ideally a sauté pan. Brown the fillets on each side, cooking them till they are browned, by which time they will be virtually cooked through. Remove them, as they are browned, to the warmed dish. Add the sliced onions and chopped garlic to the pan and cook over a moderate heat till they are soft and beginning to turn golden brown. This should take about 10 minutes. Scoop them out of the pan and into the dish with the browned turkey fillets.

Raise the heat in the pan and add the mushrooms. Cook them till they are almost crisp – this greatly improves their flavour. Then lower the heat and add the fromage frais, salt and pepper. Cook this sauce with the mushrooms for about a minute, then pour it over the turkey and onions.

Cover the dish with a lid, and bake it in a moderately hot oven – 350°F/180°C/Gas Mark 4 – for 15 minutes. Then serve.

I like creamily mashed potatoes with chopped parsley beaten into them, and carrots and parsnips cooked together, with this dish.

Roast Lamb with Anchovies

This may sound rather odd to you, I realize, but it is a most delicious way to roast lamb. It is equally good hot as cold – my sister Camilla and I both love roasting a leg (or two, depending on numbers) to serve cold for a special occasion. I cook it the same day that it is to be eaten, and there is such a variety of vegetables and salads which embellish a cold roast leg of lamb.

Leeks, for example, can be steamed till tender, then dressed whilst still very hot with a good olive oil and plenty of chopped fresh herbs; the leeks absorb the flavours of the oil and herbs as they cool. Broccoli and cauliflower are delicious cooked and served the same way. But the garlic and anchovies give the lamb an even better flavour.

Cooking it with red wine in the roasting tin helps to keep the meat moist.

Serves about 8

1 leg of lamb, weighing about 5 lb/2.25 kg	*About 2 oz/56 g soft butter*
2 cloves of garlic	*Black pepper*
1 tin of anchovy fillets	*½ pt/285 ml red wine*

With a very sharp knife, trim as much of the fat off the lamb as you can. Stick the knife into the leg of lamb in as many places as you can. Peel the garlic cloves and cut them into thin slivers. Cut the anchovy fillets in half. (If you like you can soak them in milk for half an hour before using them.) Pat them dry if you have soaked them in milk, using absorbent kitchen paper. Stuff the slivers of garlic and the pieces of anchovy fillet in the slits in the lamb. Rub the surface of the lamb with the softened butter, and season well with black pepper. Put the leg in a roasting tin and pour the wine around.

Roast in a hot oven, 425°F/220°C/Gas Mark 7, for 40 minutes, then lower the heat to 375°F/200°C/Gas Mark 5 and continue to roast for a further 45 minutes. If the meat weighs about 5 lb/2.25 kg, this will give you pinkish meat. If you prefer your lamb more pink than this gives you, reduce the cooking time by 15 minutes. If you like it cooked through, add 15–20 minutes to the cooking time. Let the meat cool before serving.

Barbecued Sea Bass with Soya Sauce

A barbecue is always a special occasion – whatever is being grilled. We have had barbecued suppers in the Christmas holidays – at least barbecuing in the winter means that there are no midges to contend with! We can get sea bass quite easily these days, thanks to Andy Race, our superb fish merchant in Mallaig. It is a firm-fleshed white fish, and is perfect for barbecuing.

The basting sauce can be made up well in advance. Although 'light' soya sauce is sold and meant for use with fish and light meats such as chicken, I don't think it is worth buying. To me it tastes diluted, and I use 'strong' soya sauce every time.

About 4 lb/1.8 kg sea bass, gutted	*2½ fl oz/70 ml medium sherry*
For the basting sauce:	*2½ fl oz/70 ml dark soya sauce*
2 cloves of garlic, skinned, and crushed with 2 tsp salt	*¾ pt/420 ml sunflower oil*

When your barbecue coals are glowing white – no sooner because the fish will cremate rather than grill – brush the grid with oil. Mix the ingredients for the basting sauce together. Brush the fish on one side with the sauce, put this side down on the grill, and brush the uppermost side with the sauce.

Grill till the flesh is cooked, turn the fish over, and rebaste the cooked side. You may prefer to turn the fish two or three times as it cooks, but whether you cook it on one side then the other, or keep turning it, keep brushing it with the sauce. It is cooked when the flesh flakes easily.

Squid with Garlic and Parsley in Olive Oil

This is a great family favourite for a special occasion, luckily for me, not only because I, too, love squid cooked this way, but also because it is just so simple and quick to cook. The preparation of the squid can be done several hours ahead, and it is simple, once you know what to expect.

Squid can be bought ready cleaned, but although this takes all effort out of their preparation bar the actual slicing, I think they taste better when bought whole. They come in a variety of sizes, but the cleaning is the same whatever the size! If you are faintly squeamish – and I never feel squeamish with fish because they live in water – wear rubber gloves to clean them.

You will be faced with a grey-film-covered squid. Look around the open end for the end of the 'quill', so named because that is exactly what it resembles. It appears to be man-made, of plastic, but it isn't! Pull the end of this clear plastic-like quill, and the whole innard should emerge with it. Rinse it out under cold running water to clean it thoroughly. Pull off the film from the outside, and you will have a clean white tube, closed at one end. Pat it dry with kitchen paper and slice in bits about ½ inch/1.5 cm wide.

SERVES 6

4 tbsp best extra virgin olive oil	*3 tbsp finely chopped parsley*
2 lb/900 g squid, cleaned and sliced	*Plenty of freshly ground black pepper*
2 cloves of garlic, skinned and very finely chopped	*Lemon quarters to serve with the cooked squid*

Heat the oil in a wide frying or sauté pan. Add some of the squid and garlic and cook till the pieces of squid turn opaque – depending on the amount in the saucepan, this can take as little as 30 seconds. Keep one lot warm while you cook the rest. But don't overcook it, because this is what makes squid tough and chewy. It should be tender when cooked briefly.

With the last lot, stir in the chopped parsley and season with pepper. Dish this in with the already cooked squid and mix it all together well. Serve as soon as possible, pouring the olive oil from the pan over the contents of the dish.

Pheasant Breasts
with Creamy Bacon Sauce

You can substitute chicken breasts for the pheasant in this recipe. On the other hand, pheasants are ever-increasingly easy to buy, even if you don't have access to them on a ready basis. This simple recipe transforms a pheasant breast into a special occasion supper. There is no doubt that the flavours of the smoked bacon, the pheasant and the cream all enhance each other quite wonderfully! And don't be aghast at the cream in the ingredients – remember that 1 pint/570 ml is divided between six people and is single cream at that, so it isn't nearly as harmful as it might seem!

SERVES 6

6 good-sized pheasant breasts
2 tbsp plain flour, sieved
2 oz/56 g butter + 2 tbsp sunflower oil
6 rashers of smoked back bacon, trimmed of fat and cut into small dice

1 pt/570 ml single cream
Plenty of freshly ground black pepper – the bacon is usually sufficiently salty for most people's tastes

Dip the pheasant breasts in the flour, coating each side. Melt the butter and heat the oil together in a wide frying or sauté pan. Cook the pheasant breasts, browning on either side, till they are cooked through – this will take about 15 minutes. Stick a knife in the middle of one, to test that it is cooked – the juices should be clear. If they are tinged with pink, give them a bit longer.

Then remove the cooked pheasant breasts to a warmed serving dish and add the diced bacon to the pan. Cook, stirring, for 2–3 minutes, then pour in the cream, season with pepper, and let the cream bubble for a couple of minutes. Pour it and the bacon over and around the pheasant breasts in the serving dish.

Keep it warm till you are ready to serve – this is good with well-mashed potatoes, and a green vegetable.

Calves' Liver with Mousseline Potatoes, Sautéed Baby Onions and Spinach with Fried Pinenuts

I just have to include this whole supper in this chapter on Special Occasion Suppers. It was my tip-top favourite supper when I was a child. Luckily, so it was for my two sisters as well, and this is the supper we had without fail on our first night home from school, when we lived in Rome, and on the last night of the holidays. It is vital that calves' liver be cooked briefly – as with squid, it is ruined by overcooking.

SERVES 6

For the liver:
2½–3 lb/1.125–1.35 kg calves' liver, trimmed of any bits of tube and cut into as neat slices as is possible
2 oz/56 g butter + 2 tbsp sunflower oil
For the potatoes:
12 medium potatoes, peeled and each cut in half
2 oz/56 g butter
½ pt/285 ml warmed milk
Salt and freshly ground black pepper

2–3 tablespoons chopped parsley and snipped chives, mixed
For the onions:
1–1½ lb/450–675 g small onions – the little pickling ones
Butter and sunflower oil for frying
For the spinach:
3 lb/1.35 kg fresh spinach
Salt and pepper
Grated nutmeg
3 oz/84 g pinenuts
1 oz/28 g butter

Cook the liver by heating the butter and oil in a wide shallow pan – a frying pan would be ideal. When the fat is very hot, cook each piece of liver on one side till it just 'seizes', till it is firm. Turn it over, and give it about 30 seconds on the other side. Remove the pieces of liver to a warmed serving plate as you continue to cook the remainder.

Boil the potatoes in salted water till just soft, then mash them with the butter, beat in the warm milk with a wooden spoon, and season with salt and black pepper. Just before transferring them to a warm dish for serving, beat in the parsley and chives.

Skin the onions – an easy way to do this and avoid an agonizing weep as you do so is to put them into a bowl and pour boiling water over them. Leave for a couple of minutes, then slice off the ends of each onion, and the skins should pop off with no effort at all – rather like skinning tomatoes. Cook them in a frying or sauté pan in a mixture of butter and sunflower oil, shaking the pan, and cooking them till they are golden brown, and tender when you stick a fork into the biggest one.

Steam the spinach till it wilts, then chop it with a sharp knife, and season it with salt, pepper and a grating of nutmeg. Fry the pinenuts in the 1 oz/28 g of butter till golden brown and scatter them over the spinach.

The onions will keep warm without spoiling, the potatoes need only the herbs beaten into them just before serving, and the spinach and calves' liver both take seconds to cook – the pinenuts can be fried in advance – so this is not a meal which is going to take you ages in preparation, but the memory lingers on. As is so often the case, the simplest food is the best.

Baked Ham Slices in Tomato and White Wine Sauce

I first ate this whilst staying with our great friend Isobel de L'Isle, who is one of the best cooks and with whom, when we are together, I feel a real injection of inspiration! We had it, that

first time, with rice and broad beans, but it is just as delicous with
potatoes, either baked in their jackets or mashed very well, and
with virtually any green vegetable – cabbage or broccoli. The
whole thing is best made ahead, and the slices of ham reheated in
the sauce before serving.

SERVES 6

*12 small slices of baked
    ham – or 6, if the slices
    are very big*
For the sauce:
*2 onions, skinned and very
    finely chopped*
½ pt/285 ml dry white wine
¼ pt/140 ml chicken stock

*2 sprigs of fresh tarragon (if
    you can't get fresh, leave
    it out rather than use
    dried)*
salt and pepper
¼ pt/140 ml double cream
*4 tomatoes, skinned,
    deseeded and chopped
    into small dice*

Put the finely chopped onions into a saucepan with the wine and
stock and the tarragon, and simmer gently till the liquid has
reduced by half – the onions will be soft. Liquidize this, and
season with salt and pepper. When it is cold, stir in the cream,
and the diced tomatoes.

Pour the sauce over the slices of ham in an ovenproof serving
dish. Cover, and reheat to serve till the sauce is bubbling very
gently – let it bubble, but very gently, for 12 minutes. Too fast
boiling will destroy the texture of the sauce.

Creamy Mushroom, Garlic and
Bacon Sauce for Pasta

As our family would happily choose pasta (or rice) seven days a
week, this sauce turns pasta into a dish fit for a special occasion. It is
invariably chosen by one or other of our offspring for a birthday

supper, and it's simplicity itself to make as well as tasting so good –
all the tastes I, too, love. All it needs to go with it is a good mixed
green salad.

SERVES 6

---

2 oz/56 g butter + 1 tbsp
    sunflower oil
1 lb/450 g mushrooms,
    wiped, stalks cut off
    level with the caps,
    and the mushrooms
    chopped
2 cloves of garlic, skinned
    and finely chopped
6 rashers smoked bacon,

grilled till just beginning
    to crisp, then chopped
    into bits
Salt and freshly ground
    black pepper
3 oz/84 g dried pasta per
    person
½ pt/285 ml single cream
2 tbsp finely chopped
    parsley

Heat the oil and melt the butter together in a wide saucepan and
cook the mushrooms and garlic together, stirring over a high heat,
till the mushrooms are almost crisp. Stir the chopped cooked bacon
in with the mushrooms, and season with a pinch of salt and lots of
freshly ground black pepper.

Meanwhile, cook the pasta in a pan with plenty of boiling salted
water, cooking it till when you push a – clean – thumbnail into a bit
it is just tender, no more. Drain it, and pour in the cream. Stir in the
mushrooms and bacon (and garlic!) and the chopped parsley, and
serve immediately.

Peanut Chicken

This is an extraordinary recipe, combining as it does peanuts with
red peppers and tomatoes. We love it, and it is a convenient dish in
that it can be cooked and will then sit without spoiling in a low
temperature oven.

I like to serve boiled Basmati rice with it, and I always like courgettes, sautéed with garlic, as an accompanying vegetable.

SERVES 6

---

6 chicken breast pieces, with the skin on	2 tomatoes, skinned, cut in quarters and the seeds scooped away
1 pt/570 ml water	8 oz/225 g roasted peanuts
Juice of half a lemon	2 tsp sesame oil
2 red peppers	A pinch of salt (the peanuts are salty) and lots of freshly ground black pepper
1 oz/28 g butter + 3 tbsp sunflower oil	
2 onions, skinned and very thinly sliced	

Put the chicken breasts in a roasting tin with the water and lemon juice. Cook them in a moderate oven, 350°F/200°C/Gas Mark 4, till they are done – about 45 minutes. Set aside the liquid and put the cooked breasts in a heatproof serving dish.

Meanwhile, prepare the peppers by cutting each in half, scooping away the seeds, and then grilling the four halves, skin uppermost, till the skin bubbles up and blackens. Then put the peppers in a polythene bag and leave for 10 minutes. The skins will peel off easily. Chop the flesh.

Heat the oil and butter in a frying or sauté pan and add the sliced onions. Cook them, stirring from time to time, till they are soft and beginning to turn golden. Add the chopped peppers and cook for a couple of minutes. Liquidize this mixture with the skinned de-seeded tomatoes, the peanuts, sesame oil, ½ pint/285 ml of the water the chicken was cooked in, and the salt and pepper. Pour this sauce over the chicken breasts.

Reheat in a moderate oven, till the sauce gently bubbles. Bubble very gently for 10 minutes before serving.

Peppered Steak with Stilton and Chive Butter

I must give credit to the New Club in Edinburgh for this special supper dish. We eat an inordinate amount of ground black pepper, and the coarser the grind, the better. So you can imagine how much we love anything au poivre. I crush black peppercorns with the end of a rolling pin, or in my pestle and mortar, and press them on to either side of the steaks, and then fry the meat in a non-stick frying pan with a very small amount of olive oil.

The Stilton and chive butter can be made two or three days in advance and kept, rolled in greaseproof paper, ready to slice in rounds about ¼ inch/½ cm thick straight from the fridge, and a piece put on top of each cooked steak.

SERVES 6

6 pieces of fillet steak (this is for a very *special occasion!)*	*2 tbsp olive oil*
	For the butter:
About 2 tbsp black peppercorns, crushed to the degree of fineness that you like	*3 oz/84 g butter*
	2 oz/56 g Stilton
	2 tsp snipped chives

Beat together the butter, Stilton and chives till they are very well mixed. Roll into a fat sausage shape between sheets of greaseproof paper and put in the fridge.

Pepper the steaks and cook them in the olive oil to the degree of doneness that each family member likes – these vary vastly in our family, from being so rare as to only need passing through the kitchen on a plate, this for Godfrey and Meriel (our third daughter), to medium cooked for the remaining four of us.

Just before serving, slice the butter evenly and put a piece on top of each steak.

Stir-Fried Monkfish with Jerusalem Artichokes, Ginger and Garlic

This is a stir-fried dish with quite delicious tastes – they are each delicious individually, but together I think they are sublime. If you prepare the artichokes ahead of time, toss the fine slices in a little lemon juice to help prevent them discolouring. The monkfish is just so ideal for stir-frying, because it keeps its shape so well, and its texture is that of the largest, juiciest prawns.

SERVES 6

1 lb/450g Jerusalem artichokes	1 oz/28g butter + 3 tbsp sunflower oil
3 medium to large monkfish tails – weight about 2 lb/ 900g	½ pt/285 ml white wine and water mixed – about half and half
A 2-in/5-cm piece of fresh ginger	2 level tsp cornflour slaked with 2 tbsp cold water
2 cloves of garlic, skinned	Salt and freshly ground black pepper

Peel and very thinly slice the artichokes. This is a fiddle, but the flavour is so well worth it I never mind. With a sharp knife, trim the membrane from the monkfish, and cut each fillet from either side of the central bone – there will be no more bones to look for. Cut each tail across in fine slices. Pare the rind from the ginger and slice both it and the skinned garlic into very thin strips, then cut them across the other way into tiny dice.

Heat the oil and melt the butter together in a wide frying or sauté pan and add the garlic and ginger, and the artichokes. Stir-fry till the slices of artichoke are soft – about 4–5 minutes – then add the monkfish. Stir-fry this in with the artichokes, ginger and garlic till the fish is opaque. Pour in the wine and water, and the cornflour mixture. Stir till the sauce bubbles. Season with salt and pepper to your taste, then tip the contents of the pan into a warmed serving dish.

Serve with boiled Basmati rice, and perhaps sugar snap peas.

Just the Family

Chicken (or Turkey, or Pheasant) Fricassée

Pot Roast Chicken with Vegetables

Grated Beetroot and Carrot Salad with Baked Potatoes and Hummus

Stir-Fried Mixed Fish with Jerusalem Artichokes

Baked Chicken with Chutney and Mustard

Slightly Curried Hot Potato, Bacon and Sultana Salad

Spinach Roulade with Lambs' Kidneys and Mushroom Filling

Winter Salad in Stilton Dressing with Baked Potatoes

Oxtail Stew

Hare Casserole with Lemon Forcemeat Balls

Kidney Casserole

Rabbit and Paprika Casserole

Minced Beef Hash

Aubergine Lasagne

Chickpea and Vegetable Stew

Pepper and Ham Risotto

Curry and Honey Roast Chicken

Baked Cod (or Hake) Fillets in Parsley, Garlic and Olive Oil Paste with Tomatoes

Baked Chicken in Tomato, Tarragon and Mustard Cream

Prosciutto, Chicken and Pasta Salad with Sun-Dried Tomatoes

Diced Fish Marinated in Fromage Frais with Herbs

Scallop and Leek Salad

Tomato and Basil Mould with Egg, Feta Cheese and Crispy Bacon

Smoked Haddock Roulade with Egg, Cheese and Parsley Filling

Salami, Apple, Celery and New Potato Salad

Three Bean, Chive and Tomato Salad with Egg Mayonnaise

Spinach, Bacon, Avocado and Feta Cheese Salad

Black Olive, Garlic, Parsley and Tomato Pasta

Red Onion and Red Pepper Tart with Cheese Pastry

Spinach and Goats' Cheese Tart

Smoked Haddock and Parsley Mousse

Vegetable and Cheese Millefeuille

Meatballs with Tomato Sauce and Spinach Purée

Casseroled Pork with Vegetables and Soya Sauce

Pork Chops with Apples, Onions and Cider

Ham Terrine

Braised Brisket with Root Vegetables

Casseroled Beef with Mushrooms and Black Olives

Pork Chops with Onions and Oranges

Sausagemeat Puff Pastry Plate Pie

Cheese and Tomato Pudding

Broccoli and Mushroom Risotto

Chicken Stew with Parsley and Chive Dumplings

JUST THE FAMILY

There can't be a more repeated or more plaintive cry in this household than my near-daily refrain of 'What shall we have for supper?'! I can think of what to put on the menu for our hotel guests with comparative ease, but I am just dry, inspiration-wise, when it comes to feeding our family. And it is such a ridiculous question to ask when there are four children and a husband, because, of course, everyone gives a different answer, and then no-one can agree. It is easier when we have family or friends visiting us – perhaps this is because it is simpler to think of things to cook which are rather more out of the ordinary, for a special occasion.

The criteria for feeding a family – our family, anyway – are simplicity, coupled with healthy eating, and added to these must be cost. In several instances it can incorporate leftovers, as in the recipe for Chicken (or Turkey, or Pheasant) Fricassée, a dish which can cause people to shudder at the mere mention of the word fricassée, because so often this means a stodgy white sauce with chopped chicken, or whatever, stirred into it. Most unappetizing. A well-made fricassée is full of flavour and quite delicious. I think that interest in eating, and then follows an interest in cooking, stems from what children eat at home, in fact, when it is 'just the family'. So I feel that what we cook should matter just as much when it is just the family as it does for occasions when we are more than just the family!

Variety is the key, and also, from an early age, to give children dishes containing garlic, small amounts of curry powder, spices and herbs, and things like mushrooms and even cheeses such as Stilton. These are all categories of food which children can love, provided they have been introduced to their tastes from an early age, and being able to cook with a wide range of ingredients and flavours makes the task of the mother, or provider of food whoever he or she may be, so very much easier.

Another type of supper dish which greatly appeals to me is the one-dish meal. Examples in this chapter include the Smoked Haddock Roulade and the Spinach Roulade, and the pasta, salads, risottos and Vegetable Millefeuille recipes, to name but a few. These all need either nothing else at all, or just a salad to accompany them.

What you cook depends to a great extent on the seasons. For instance, I couldn't think of cooking and eating an oxtail stew in July, never mind how chilly the weather. And then there are several recipes which can be made, eaten and enjoyed whatever the season – dishes like Spinach and Goats' Cheese Tart, Pork Chops with Onions and Oranges, and Curry and Honey Roast Chicken. There are several recipes for non-meat-eaters in this chapter – like Chickpea and Vegetable Stew, Three Bean, Chive and Tomato Salad with Egg Mayonnaise, Red Onion and Red Pepper Tart with Cheese Pastry and Cheese and Tomato Pudding. Along with very many other families throughout Britain, we seem to eat meat far less than we used to do, not in any conscious way in our case, just through a sort of evolvement of eating habits.

So I very much hope that if you, like me, are wondering what on earth to give your family for supper this evening, you may find some help within this chapter!

Chicken (or Turkey, or Pheasant) Fricassée

A fricassée is viewed by some as a sort of dustbin dish. This view is taken by those for whom a fricassée means a thick white sauce containing chopped leftover chicken (or turkey) – and chopped chicken which hasn't been carefully trimmed of gristle and other unappetizing bits of skin and fat, a trimming most important to make a good and appealing fricassée.

This is the way I make a fricassée, and a pheasant fricassée is the very first thing I cooked by myself. I think it is essential to have leftover fat from the roasting tin, and the jellied juices which you will find under the fat – both have all the flavour of the chicken and, if the bird was stuffed, of the stuffings too.

SERVES 6

---

3 tbsp (approx.) dripping
from the roasting tin

2 medium onions, skinned
and finely chopped

2 sticks celery, washed,
trimmed and very finely
sliced

3 rashers of back bacon,
trimmed of most of its fat
and sliced

2 carrots, peeled and
chopped into very small
dice

2 teaspoons medium curry
powder (this isn't enough
to be detected

by avowed curry haters)

2 oz/56 g flour

1¼ pts/710 ml chicken
stock, or 1 pt/570 ml + 2–
3 tbsp jellied stock from
the roasting tin

2 oz/56 g raisins or sultanas
(optional, but I always
add them)

Salt and ground black
pepper

About 1 lb/450 g chopped,
trimmed leftover chicken
or pheasant – more, if
possible; if less, use an
extra carrot

Put the dripping into a saucepan and add the finely chopped onions, finely sliced celery and bacon, and finely diced carrots. Cook all together for about 8–10 minutes, stirring from time to time to prevent the vegetables and bacon from sticking, and to make sure that they cook evenly. Stick a fork into a bit of carrot – it should feel just tender. If it doesn't, cook for a further few minutes. The carrots are the part of this mixture which need most cooking, and as they won't get any length of cooking time after this stage they need to be cooked through now.

Stir in the curry powder, then the flour, and cook for a minute or two before pouring in the stock, gradually, and stirring continuously till the sauce bubbles. Stir in the raisins, and season with salt and pepper. If you intend to eat this immediately, stir in the chopped chicken (or pheasant, or turkey, whichever you are using) and reheat gently, in the saucepan, letting the sauce bubble very gently for 10 minutes. Don't let it boil fast because that will reduce your leftover chicken to shreds – not the aim. If you want to make up the mixture in advance, let it cool completely before adding the leftover chicken, to avoid reheating it more than once.

Serve with boiled Basmati rice, and a mixture of cooked root vegetables such as julienne strips of parsnip, Jerusalem artichokes and celeriac, or with a green vegetable like courgettes sautéed in olive oil with chopped garlic. Or, if you have tastes like my family (what an admission, this), with frozen peas cooked with mint and half a teaspoon of sugar.

Pot Roast Chicken with Vegetables

As our family would happily eat chicken six times a week, this is a useful recipe in my repertoire. Any leftover makes delicious soup for lunch the next day. The better the chicken, the better will be the dish – I try to buy free-range poultry as a rule. With a dish like this, a chicken weighing upwards of 3½ lb/1.6 kg will feed a family of six, because the quantities are padded out with the vegetables; otherwise I find I need two chickens for straight roasting.

SERVES 6

---

4 tbsp olive oil
1 chicken, weighing approx. 3½ lb/1.6 kg – more, not less
3 onions, skinned and neatly chopped
2 cloves of garlic, skinned and finely chopped
4 sticks of celery, washed, trimmed and sliced

2 leeks, washed, trimmed and sliced
Two 15-oz/420-g tins of chopped tomatoes
2 tsp pesto
Salt and ground black pepper
½ tsp sugar
½ pt/285 ml chicken stock

In a heavy casserole, heat the oil and brown the chicken all over. When it's browned, take it out of the hot oil and put it on to a warmed plate or dish. Put the chopped onions into the casserole and cook them, stirring occasionally, for 5 minutes – they will be soft and transparent-looking. Then stir in the garlic, celery and leeks, and continue to cook for a further 5 minutes. Lastly, stir in the contents of the tins of tomatoes, the pesto, salt, pepper, sugar and stock. Stir till the mixture bubbles, then put the chicken back into the casserole, pushing it down among the vegetables in the sauce.

Cover the casserole with its lid, and cook in a moderate oven, 350°F/180°C/Gas Mark 4, for 1 hour. Stick the sharp point of a knife into the chicken's thigh – if the juices run clear, the chicken is cooked. If they are tinged with pink, continue to cook it for a further 10–15 minutes.

When the chicken is cooked, lift it on to a board or plate and carve it, spooning the vegetables and sauce over the slices. I like to serve this with creamily mashed potatoes or baked potatoes, and a green vegetable – courgettes are especially good with this.

Grated Beetroot and Carrot Salad with Baked Potatoes and Hummus

It is rare to come across grated raw beetroot, but it is so delicious and combines very well with grated carrots in a salad which makes for very good winter suppers. The only thing against grating beetroot is that, whilst peeling and grating, the beetroot inevitably dyes your fingers a handsome shade of burgundy, but as this washes off quite easily it seems a small deterrent. Dressed with a spoonful of French dressing, and served with baked jacket potatoes and hummus, this is a really good supper at any time of the year, but especially for winter months. It is quick to prepare, and everything can be done in advance – potatoes scrubbed all ready to be popped into the oven to cook.

SERVES 6

1 large potato per person, or more depending on appetites	*¹⁄₄ pt/140 ml tahini paste – this is sesame seed paste*
3 beetroot, each about the size of a cricket ball	*2 large cloves of garlic, blanched in their skins for 1 minute*
5–6 medium carrots	*¹⁄₄ pt/140 ml olive oil + 1 tbsp lemon juice*
2 oz/56 g raisins – optional	
2 oz/56 g chopped walnuts – optional	*Salt and plenty of freshly ground black pepper to your taste*
French dressing, with 1 tsp medium curry powder shaken in	*¹⁄₄ pt/140 ml fromage frais*
For the hummus:	*2 tbsp finely chopped parsley – this 'lifts' the colour of the hummus, as well as adding its fresh flavour*
6 oz/170 g dried chickpeas, soaked overnight	
1 clove of garlic, skinned	

The hummus can be made a day or more in advance and kept, covered, in the fridge till supper-time.

Simmer the chickpeas with a skinned clove of garlic for 1½–2 hours. Drain any excess liquid off them before putting them into a food processor. Add the tahini. Snip the ends off the blanched cloves of garlic and squeeze – the garlic should pop out of its skin into the processor. Whiz, adding the olive oil drop by drop at first (as for making mayonnaise), then in a thin trickle. Whiz in the lemon juice, season with salt and pepper, and whiz in the fromage frais and the parsley. Spoon and scrape this into a serving bowl.

Scrub the potatoes, and stab each right through with a knife – this helps them to cook rather more quickly, at the same time as preventing them from bursting during cooking, as occasionally happens. If you like, rub each potato with a very small amount of oil – sunflower oil – and roll each potato in rock salt. This is purely optional.

Bake in a hot oven, depending on the size, for 45–60 minutes. Press the largest potato, it should feel soft when cooked. Set the oven at 400°F/200°C/Gas Mark 6, or use the top oven in an Aga or Raeburn.

For the salad, grate the peeled beetroot and carrots into a bowl, and stir in the raisins and chopped walnuts (if you are using them). Toss with the curry French dressing – you can dress this salad well in advance, unlike a green salad. In fact I think it is nicest dressed well ahead, so that the grated vegetables marinate in the dressing.

Stir-Fried Mixed Fish with Jerusalem Artichokes

Any stir-fried dish takes literally minutes – usually less than 5 – to actually cook, even if the preparation takes rather longer. But the preparation can all be done well in advance, in the morning, ready for the quick cooking before supper. I like to serve a mixed green salad with this, and boiled Basmati rice. The mixture of fish can be whatever you have to hand. It needn't be a mixture, but can be just one type of fish – hake, for example. Or you can use a mixture of hake and monkfish, and add some chopped scallops too.

SERVES 6

3 tbsp sunflower oil

1 in/2.5 cm fresh root ginger, peeled and finely chopped

About 12 spring onions, trimmed and finely sliced

1 lb/450 g Jerusalem artichokes, each peeled and sliced into fine slivers; toss them in lemon juice, to help prevent discolouring

1½ lb/675 g firm-fleshed white fish, e.g. hake or monkfish, skinned, bones removed, and fish cut into bits about 1 in/2.5 cm in size

6 scallops (their flavour goes especially well with the Jerusalem artichokes), each scallop cut in half

*2 tbsp each of: Hoisin sauce,
dark or strong soya
sauce, and dry sherry (the
Hoisin sauce is to be
found on most
supermarket shelves, and
I don't bother with 'light'
soya sauce, even*

*though it is meant for use
with fish and chicken – it
tastes dilute and wishy-
washy)*
*Freshly ground black
pepper – the soya sauce
should provide enough
saltiness*

Having cooked the rice, 5 minutes before you want to eat supper heat the oil in a wok or large frying or sauté pan. When it is very hot, add the ginger and spring onions, and the prepared artichokes, and stir-fry them for a couple of minutes. Then stir in the prepared fish and scallops. Cook them till the pieces of fish turn opaque – a minute or two. Then stir in the Hoisin sauce, soya sauce and sherry, and the pepper. Cook for a further minute, then serve – simple!

Baked Chicken
with Chutney and Mustard

This is one of those extremely easy dishes, and one that tastes very good. The sooner the chicken breasts are smeared with the chutney mixture, the better – in the morning for supper that evening, or, even better, the previous day and kept, covered, in the fridge. The mustard used is grainy mustard, and the chutney I use is mango, but I don't see why you couldn't substitute any other type of fruity chutney. It is essential to use chicken breasts which have their skin on – the skinless type dry out during cooking.

This is good served with a green vegetable, such as steamed broccoli or stir-fried cabbage, and mashed potatoes.

6 tbsp chutney (mango, for example)	*6 tbsp olive oil*
3 tbsp grainy mustard (moutarde de Meaux)	*6 chicken breasts with their skin on*

Mix the chutney, mustard and oil together and smear this mixture over the chicken breasts in an ovenproof dish. Do this several hours in advance, and keep the dish, covered, in the fridge. An hour before cooking, take the dish out of the fridge and leave in room temperature.

Bake in a hot oven, 400°F/200°C/Gas Mark 6, for 25 minutes – stab a chicken breast and check that the juices which run from it are clear to see if it is cooked through. This cooking time is right for the average-sized chicken breast. If you think the mixture is getting rather too brown for your liking, put a piece of greaseproof paper (or a butter paper) over the top.

Slightly Curried Hot Potato, Bacon and Sultana Salad

I love the combination of flavours and textures in this rather unusual warm dish, but I have to come clean and admit that two of our four children loathe it! But they don't like sultanas in savoury food, and this is one recipe where I feel they belong, so I am not prepared to compromise and put 'optional' after them in the list of ingredients, and nor do I leave them out when making this for us for supper – I just choose to make it when the two non-appreciators are away from home! It is good served with a crunchy green salad based on either finely shredded cabbage or Chinese leaves.

SERVES 6

---

2 lb/900 g potatoes, peeled, and boiled till just tender; drain well, and chop the potatoes into chunks between 1 in/2.5 cm and 2 in/5cm in size	For the dressing:
	4–5 tbsp olive oil
	1 tsp medium curry powder
	1 tsp runny honey
	½ tsp salt and plenty of ground black pepper
3 oz/84 g sultanas	*1 clove of garlic, skinned and very finely chopped*
6 rashers of smoked back bacon, grilled till crisp, then chopped small	*1 tbsp wine vinegar (white or red, it doesn't matter)*
	2 tbsp finely chopped parsley

Mix all together well, and serve warm rather than hot.

Spinach Roulade with Lambs' Kidneys and Mushroom Filling

A similar recipe to this one is in my first book, *Seasonal Cooking*, but I think it is such a delicious and useful dish that I make no apologies for including it here. It is a good combination of complementary tastes and flavours – the spinach goes so well with the kidneys and mushrooms, and the nutmeg in the spinach enhances the lot. It is a useful recipe because it is one of those dishes where the whole course is in one.

If you like, you can serve baked potatoes or warm granary bread as an accompaniment, if you are feeding vast appetites. Otherwise, I don't bother with any other accompaniment.

The recipe for the actual spinach roulade here is slightly different – I have improved the texture by adding the Philadelphia to the spinach.

SERVES 6

For the roulade:
2 lb/900 g frozen leaf
   spinach, well drained
   when thawed
1 oz/28 g butter
1 clove of garlic, skinned
   and chopped
A 3-oz/84-g carton of
   Philadelphia cream
   cheese, or a low fat
   alternative such as Shape
   or Light
4 large eggs, separated
Salt and freshly ground
   black pepper

A grating of nutmeg
For the filling:
2 oz/56 g butter
6 lambs' kidneys, cored and
   chopped
½ lb/225 g mushrooms,
   wiped and chopped
2 oz/56 g flour
1 pt/570 ml milk
6 rashers of smoked or
   unsmoked back bacon,
   grilled till crisp, then
   chopped in quite small
   bits

Line a shallow baking tray or roasting tin with siliconized grease-proof paper, the tin measuring about 12 by 14 inches/30 by 35 cm.

Put the spinach into a food processor with the butter, garlic and Philadelphia, and whiz till smooth, gradually adding the egg yolks, one by one. Season with the salt, pepper and nutmeg. In a bowl, whisk the egg whites with a pinch of salt – to give increased volume – till they are very stiff, then, with a large metal spoon, quickly and thoroughly fold them through the spinach mixture. Pour and scrape this into the paper-lined baking tin, and smooth evenly.

Bake in a moderate oven, 350°F/180°C/Gas Mark 4, till firm to the touch, 15–20 minutes. Take the tin out of the oven, cover it with a damp teatowel and leave it for 2–3 minutes. Then, holding the shorter ends of the paper under the spinach in either hand, tip it face down on to a fresh piece of siliconized paper on a work surface. Carefully peel off the paper from the back of the roulade, tearing in straight strips parallel with the long sides of the roulade. This avoids tearing the roulade up with the paper.

You can make the filling while the spinach is cooking. Melt the butter and cook the chopped kidneys in it till just firm. Scoop them out of the butter and on to a warmed dish. Add the chopped mushrooms to the butter and cook for a minute, then stir in the flour. Cook for a minute, then gradually add the milk, stirring continuously. Stir till the sauce boils, then take the pan off the heat. Stir in the cooked kidneys and the bits of bacon, and season with salt and pepper.

Spread this filling over the spinach, and carefully roll up the roulade, rolling away from you, and slip it on to a warmed serving plate or ashet. Serve as soon as possible – it will keep warm without spoiling for up to 10 minutes or so, but the sooner it is eaten, the nicer it will be.

Winter Salad in Stilton Dressing with Baked Potatoes

As our family all love baked potatoes, I have discovered over the years that they can form the main part of supper, provided they are accompanied by a good and flavour-packed salad. Salad used to mean a summer-time dish, but I am increasingly discovering that winter vegetables adapt as good salad ingredients every bit as much as the summer lettuces of all different types. And the other aspect of suppers such as this one is that they are so healthy. They make good contrasts to the more usual stews and casseroles that we tend to eat in the winter evenings.

SERVES 6

As many potatoes as you think necessary – I reckon 1 large potato per person, or 2 if there are vast appetites

For the salad:
1 Savoy cabbage
½ head of Chinese leaves
2 oranges

3 good eating apples, e.g. Cox's
4 spring onions, trimmed and sliced
3–4 tbsp French dressing

For the Stilton dressing:
12 oz/340 g Stilton
4 tbsp milk
1 tbsp snipped chives (if you have them)

Scrub the potatoes. Rub each one with a very small amount of sunflower oil, if you like, and roll each potato in rock salt. This is optional. Stab each potato right through – this prevents it from bursting during baking. It also helps it cook slightly quicker.

Bake the potatoes in a hot oven, 400°F/200°C/Gas Mark 6, for 45–60 minutes, depending on the size of the potatoes.

Trim the Savoy cabbage and slice it very finely – this doesn't take a minute, provided you have a good board and a very sharp knife. Do the same with the Chinese leaves. Put the shredded cabbage and leaves into a salad bowl. With a serrated knife, cut the skin off the oranges and chop them, removing any pips. Put the chopped oranges and their juice into the salad bowl. Cut each apple into four, cut out the core (leave the skins on) and chop each cored quarter. Put them into the salad bowl and toss everything in the French dressing.

To make the Stilton dressing, put the Stilton into a processor and whiz, adding the milk gradually. Scrape this mixture into a serving dish and stir in the snipped chives.

The taste of the Stilton goes very well with the contents of the salad, as well as with the baked potatoes.

Oxtail Stew

For me, this is the best of all stews and casseroles. Oxtail is such succulent, rich meat. It does need long slow cooking, and, like all casseroles and stews, it benefits from being made, cooled, and reheated to serve. The flavours seem to intensify with this reheating.

I like it best of all served with baked potatoes (and there is no need to have butter with the potatoes when they are accompanying oxtail stew, although Godfrey disagrees with this!) and steamed cabbage.

My only word of warning is never to buy frozen oxtails. Unlike most bits of meat, oxtails just don't freeze well, they deteriorate in both flavour and texture. The ready-made stew, on the other hand, freezes very well.

SERVES 6

2 oxtails
4 tbsp sunflower oil
3 medium onions, skinned and fairly finely chopped
3 carrots, each peeled and neatly sliced, either in slices or julienne strips
4 parsnips (their flavour seems to enhance that of the oxtail, as does

the turnip), peeled and sliced or cut into julienne strips
½ average turnip, skin cut off and chopped
3 tbsp flour
2 tbsp tomato purée
1 can of lager
1½ pts/850 ml water
2 pinches of dried thyme
Salt and freshly ground black pepper

With a sharp knife, cut off all possible fat from the pieces of oxtail. Fill a large saucepan with water and bring it to the boil. Put the trimmed pieces of oxtail into the boiling water, bring the water back to boiling point, then drain well. Pat the bits of oxtail dry with absorbent kitchen paper.

In a large and heavy casserole, heat the oil and brown the pieces of blanched oxtail on all sides, removing them to a warm dish. Lower the heat a bit, and add the chopped onions. Cook them, stirring occasionally to prevent them sticking, for about 5 minutes. Then add the prepared carrots, parsnips and turnip and cook for 7–10 minutes, stirring from time to time. Although this part of making the oxtail stew seems rather lengthy, I urge you not to try to curtail it by bunging everything in at once, because it – the inital cooking of the onions, for example – really does contribute towards the overall flavour of the end result.

Stir in the flour, let it cook for a minute, then stir in the tomato purée, the lager and the water, stirring till the sauce around the vegetables bubbles. Add the thyme, and salt and pepper, and replace the pieces of browned oxtail in the casserole, pushing them down amongst the vegetables.

Cover with a lid, and cook in an oven temperature 300°F/150°C/ Gas Mark 3 for 2½–3 hours. Cool completely, skim any surplus fat from the surface, cover, and store in a fridge or cold larder. Bring the casserole into room temperature for an hour before putting it into a moderate oven, 350°F/180°C/Gas Mark 4, and cooking it for 1–1¼ hours before serving. The meat should be falling from the bones.

Any leftover oxtail stew can either be frozen and eaten at a later date when you are alone, or whizzed into delicious oxtail soup, thinned down with stock to a soup consistency.

Hare Casserole with Lemon Forcemeat Balls

Forcemeat balls freeze beautifully, and can be made in batches and kept in the freezer, thawing and reheating them to serve with this casserole and with other gamey dishes. I love hare, always feeling hypocritical because I love them alive, too. But hare (and rabbit) is good for you, inexpensive, and it is such a good thing to make the most of food like game when it is available to us. If you can get the blood, so much the better, it enriches the sauce as in the classical dish *Jugged Hare*.

SERVES 6

4 tbsp sunflower oil
1 large hare, cut into joints
3 onions, skinned and thinly sliced
3 parsnips, peeled and cut into neat julienne strips
3 carrots, peeled and cut into neat julienne strips
½ turnip, skin cut off and the turnip neatly chopped

2 cloves of garlic, skinned and finely chopped
4 juniper berries, crushed with the end of a rolling pin
3 tbsp flour
Grated rind of ½ orange and ½ lemon, both well scrubbed and dried before grating
½ pt/285 ml red wine

1½ pts/850 ml water
½ tsp dried thyme
2 tsp redcurrant jelly
Salt and ground black
pepper
Blood of the hare, if you
have it
For the forcemeat balls:
2 oz/56 g butter and 1 tbsp
sunflower oil
2 medium onions, skinned
and very finely chopped
6 oz/170 g white
breadcrumbs (made from
baked, not steamed
bread)

1 tbsp finely chopped
parsley – whiz this in the
processor with the bread
when you are making the
crumbs
3 oz/84 g shredded suet
Grated rind of 1 well
washed and dried lemon
Salt and ground black
pepper
1 beaten egg
Flour in which to roll the
balls before frying
Sunflower oil for frying

In a large casserole, heat the oil and brown the pieces of hare on each side, removing them as they brown to a warmed serving dish. Lower the heat a bit and add the sliced onions to the casserole, cooking them, stirring occasionally, for 5 minutes. Stir in the prepared parsnips, carrots, turnip and garlic, and the juniper berries, stirring occasionally. Stir in the flour, let it cook for a minute, then stir in the grated orange and lemon rinds, the wine and water, thyme, redcurrant jelly, salt and pepper. Stir this till it comes to bubbling point, then replace the browned pieces of hare, pushing them down amongst the vegetables.

Cover the casserole with its lid, and cook in an oven at 300°F/ 150°C/Gas Mark 3 for 2 hours. Cool the casserole and fish out the hare. Cut the meat off the bones and put it back into the sauce and vegetables. Cover, and store in a fridge or larder till you are ready to reheat before serving.

Reheat by bringing the casserole to room temperature for an hour, then putting it into a moderate oven, 350°F/180°C/Gas Mark 4, and cooking for 45–50 minutes. Add the hare's blood to the casserole just before serving by mixing it with a small amount of the hot sauce, then stirring this into the sauce. Don't let it boil again after the blood is added.

To make the forcemeat balls, melt the butter and heat the oil together in a saucepan, add the finely chopped onion, and cook till the onion is very soft and transparent-looking. Cool. Then stir this into the breadcrumbs, parsley, suet, grated lemon rind, salt and pepper. Stir in the egg to bind it all together.

Form the mixture into balls about the size of a large walnut, roll each in flour, and store on a tray lined with siliconized baking parchment. If you want to freeze them, do so at this stage.

Before serving, heat a small amount of sunflower oil in a non-stick frying pan and fry the forcemeat balls, turning them so that they become golden brown all over.

I love the lemoniness of these with the hare!

Kidney Casserole

For this you need ox kidney. Lambs' kidneys are ruined when cooked for any longer than a brief sautéeing in either bacon fat or butter. Yet the flavour of kidneys is a delicious one, and enhanced by mushrooms, and by Madeira, as in this recipe. One taste I don't like with kidney is tomato.

I think this casserole is nicest served with very creamily mashed potatoes, with chopped parsley beaten into them just before serving, and with cauliflower in a creamy white sauce seasoned with nutmeg.

SERVES 6

2 lb/900 g ox kidney	³/₄ lb/340 g mushrooms,
6 rashers of back bacon – I	wiped and chopped,
prefer to use smoked	stalks cut off even with
bacon	the caps
2 tbsp sunflower oil + 2 oz/	2 tbsp flour
56 g butter	1¹/₄ pts/710 ml water
1 medium onion, skinned	¹/₄ pt/140 ml Madeira
and very finely chopped	Salt and ground black
	pepper to your taste

With a very sharp knife, cut the kidney from the central core, cutting the meat into bits as even in size as possible – there will be some bits which will be very small, you can't help it. Cut as much as you possibly can from the core. Cut the fat from the bacon, and cut it into strips.

Heat the oil and melt the butter together in a casserole and put the chopped bacon and kidney into the fat, stirring till it browns. Scoop this mixture into a warmed dish and cook the chopped onion, stirring occasionally, for about 3–5 minutes, till the onion looks transparent. Scoop this out and into the dish with the kidneys and bacon. Raise the heat under the casserole and cook the chopped mushrooms till they are almost crisp – this greatly improves their flavour. Lower the heat, stir in the flour, cook for a minute, then stir in the water. Stir till this sauce boils, then stir in the Madeira, a little salt and lots of ground black pepper. Replace the kidneys, bacon and onions in amongst the mushroom.

Cover with a lid, and cook in a moderate oven, 350°F/200°C/Gas Mark 4, for 40–45 minutes before serving. You can make this in advance, in which case only cook it for 30 minutes, and reheat it for 20 minutes in a moderate oven.

Rabbit and Paprika Casserole

You can buy rabbit in most supermarkets and butchers' shops, and whereas you can use chicken instead of rabbit in this recipe, it does seem a waste not to use rabbit when we can now get it, wherever we live, whether in the middle of a city or in the depths of the country. I think that on the whole, rabbit benefits from casserole type of cooking rather than the sauté type.

In this casserole the pieces of rabbit are browned, then cooked in the sauce. When cooked the casserole is cooled, and the rabbit is cut off the bones and reheated in the sauce with soured cream or fromage frais added.

I like to serve this with pasta, like green tagliatelle, and spinach.

SERVES 6

6 joints of rabbit	*1–2 cloves of garlic,*
2 tbsp flour mixed with 1	*skinned and finely*
tsp salt and plenty of	*chopped*
black pepper	*1 tbsp paprika*
4 tbsp sunflower oil	*1½ pts/850 ml chicken*
2 onions, skinned and finely	*stock*
chopped	*¼ pt/140 ml fromage frais*
	(or soured cream)

Coat the joints of rabbit with the seasoned flour. Heat the oil in a large casserole and brown the pieces of rabbit on each side, removing them as they brown to a warmed dish. Lower the heat a bit and add the chopped onions to the casserole. Cook them, stirring occasionally to prevent them from sticking, till they are just beginning to turn golden at the edges, about 5–7 minutes. Then add the chopped garlic, any remaining flour and the paprika, and stir for a minute before adding the stock, stirring continuously till this sauce boils. Replace the browned pieces of rabbit in the sauce.

Cover with a lid, and bake in a moderate oven, 350°F/180°C/Gas Mark 4, for 1–1¼ hours. Take the dish out of the oven, cool, strip the meat from the bones and reheat it in the sauce. Just before serving, stir in the fromage frais, or soured cream, reheating the sauce gently and trying not to let it boil after the fromage frais is added. Taste, and add more salt and pepper if you think it is needed. (Reheat it in a moderate oven till the sauce bubbles gently – let it simmer very gently for 10 minutes before adding the fromage frais.)

Minced Beef Hash

I much prefer to 'mince' my own beef, that way I know exactly what goes into it, and can trim just about all the fat and definitely all the gristle from it before I put it into the processor and whiz it to the stage where it is coarse, but not pulverized. This mixture is convenient in that it can be made in advance and reheated. It can be frozen without deteriorating in either taste or texture.

It is good served with baked potatoes and a salad, or it can be served with pasta, the short shapes such as shells or bows, tossed in a tablespoonful or two or cream and some chopped parsley.

SERVES 6

---

2 lb/900 g rump steak, trimmed of fat (the meat, if it is good meat, will be marbled with fat to keep it succulent) and any gristle
3 tbsp sunflower or olive oil
2 onions, skinned and finely chopped
1–2 cloves of garlic,

skinned and finely chopped
1 tbsp flour
2 tbsp tomato purée
2 tsp redcurrant jelly
1½ pts/850 ml water and red wine – I leave the ratio up to you
1 tbsp Worcestershire sauce
Salt and ground black pepper

Put the trimmed meat, cut in chunks, into the processor and whiz briefly till it is coarsely chopped – not pulverized.

Heat the oil in a heavy sauté pan and brown the meat, over a fairly high heat. Scoop it into a warmed dish, draining off as much oil as you can as you scoop. Lower the heat and put the chopped onions into the pan. Cook, stirring, for about 4–5 minutes, till the onions are just turning golden at their edges. Halfway through the onions' cooking time, add the chopped garlic – if you add it too soon, it will lose too much of its taste. Then stir in the flour and tomato purée, and the redcurrant jelly, wine and water mixture and Worcestershire sauce, and stir till this sauce boils.

Season with salt and pepper, stir the meat into the oniony sauce, and simmer very gently, with the pan uncovered, for about 20 minutes. Try not to let it bubble fast, because this will make the mixture stick on the bottom of the sauté pan – just a very gentle heaving of the mixture is all that is needed!

Either serve immediately, or cool and store in the fridge, covered, and reheat gently till it 'heaves'. Let it cook very gently for 10 minutes, then serve.

Aubergine Lasagne

This has slices of fried aubergine instead of the sheets of pasta which constitute a proper lasagne. If you think, as I used to, that frying aubergines requires a vat of oil, then read on . . . I discovered a year or two ago that by dipping the slices of aubergine first in sieved flour then in beaten egg (yes, I really do mean in that order!) they absorb a scant amount of oil as they fry. As with the last recipe, I really prefer to 'mince' my own beef in my food processor. You can use a lesser quality of beef than that used in the Minced Beef Hash recipe, (page 205), but then you need more of it because you will find you need to trim more fat and gristle from it. It can be made ahead and reheated to serve and it freezes.

SERVES 6

2 aubergines, sliced lengthways into slices about ¼ in/½ cm thick	1–2 cloves of garlic, skinned and finely chopped
3–4 tbsp olive oil	2 tbsp tomato purée
1½–2 lb/675–900 g beef, stewing steak or rump, trimmed of fat and gristle and 'minced' in a processor but not pulverized	A 15-oz/420-g tin chopped tomatoes
	¾ pt/420 ml red wine
	Salt and freshly ground black pepper
2 onions, skinned and finely chopped	2–3 tbsp olive oil – for cooking the aubergine slices
2 carrots, peeled and diced small	Flour to coat the aubergine slices, sieved
3 back bacon rashers, trimmed of fat and diced quite small	1 egg, beaten
	4 oz/112 g Cheddar cheese, grated

First, put the aubergine slices on a large plate or tray and sprinkle with salt – not too thickly. Leave for 20–30 minutes, then pat dry with absorbent kitchen paper – drops of brownish liquid will have appeared on the slices.

Next, make the meaty sauce by heating the first amount of oil in a saucepan and browning the minced beef, removing it as it browns to a warmed dish, with a slotted spoon to drain as much oil as is possible back into the saucepan. Lower the heat and put the chopped onions and diced carrots into the oil. Cook, stirring, for about 5 minutes, adding the bacon and garlic halfway through. Stick the point of a knife into a bit of carrot – it should feel tender. If it doesn't (people's ideas of 'fine' dice differ!) continue to cook for a further few minutes. Then stir in the tomato purée, replace the browned minced beef, and add the wine, salt and pepper. Bring this mixture to a very gentle simmer, and cook for 30 minutes, with the pan half-covered with a lid.

Meanwhile, heat the oil, dip the aubergine slices first into the sieved flour, then into the beaten egg on a plate, and fry the slices in relays in the oil in a frying or sauté pan. Take them out as they turn pale golden on each side, and put on a warmed dish with a couple of thicknesses of kitchen paper to absorb any excess oil.

Cover the base of a shallow ovenproof dish with a layer of aubergine, then with a layer of the meat mixture. Repeat the layering. Sprinkle with the grated cheese, and bake in a moderate oven, 350°F/180°C/Gas mark 4, for 25–30 minutes. The cheese should be melted and the meaty sauce bubbling gently.

This is good served with baked potatoes and a green salad.

Chickpea and Vegetable Stew

This easy dish is also convenient in that it can be made in the morning for supper that evening, or it can be made the day before and kept in the fridge overnight. It is a meal-in-one dish, really needing nothing to go with it except, possibly, a salad.

The sesame oil in the recipe is used as a seasoning – I find that sesame oil burns easily and its taste (and smell!) is so pungent and delicious that it is much better to use it as a flavouring than as a medium for sautéeing or frying.

Although you can buy tinned chickpeas, and it is very useful to have a couple of tins on your larder shelf, I prefer to use dried chickpeas. They do need to be soaked overnight and simmered for about 2 hours before being used in the recipe.

SERVES 6

---

8 oz/225 g dried chickpeas, soaked overnight

3 tbsp olive oil

2 onions, skinned and thinly sliced

1–2 cloves of garlic, skinned and finely chopped

2 sticks of celery, washed, trimmed and finely sliced

4 leeks, washed, trimmed and finely sliced on the diagonal – it looks nicer

1/2 lb/225 g mushrooms, wiped, stalks cut level with the caps, and sliced

6 courgettes, trimmed, and sliced diagonally about 1/4 in/1/2 cm thick

1 lb/450 g tomatoes, skinned, de-seeded and chopped

Salt and ground black pepper

1/2 pt/285 ml vegetable or chicken stock

2 tbsp sesame oil

4 oz/112 g sugar snap peas, sliced diagonally

Soak the chickpeas overnight, then simmer them for 2 hours. Keep topping up the water, and add half a teaspoon of salt and a skinned clove of garlic to the water as they simmer. Drain off any excess liquid.

Heat the oil in a casserole and fry the sliced onions till they are soft, transparent-looking and just beginning to turn golden at the edges. Then add the chopped garlic, celery and leeks, and cook for about 10 minutes, over moderate heat, stirring from time to time to prevent the mixture sticking. With a slotted spoon, to drain as much oil as possible back into the casserole, scoop out the contents of the casserole on to a warmed dish. If you think it needs more oil, add another tablespoonful, raise the heat and cook the mushrooms till they are almost crisp – this improves their flavour enormously. Scoop them into the warmed dish with the other vegetables, and cook the sliced courgettes in the casserole till they are soft and turning golden. This initial sautéeing is important to the flavour of the finished dish. Replace the vegetables in the casserole with the courgettes, and add the chopped tomatoes, salt, pepper, stock and sesame oil, and the drained chickpeas.

Cover the casserole with a lid and simmer or bake in a moderate oven, 350°F/180°C/Gas Mark 4, very gently for 25 minutes. Just before serving, stir in the sliced sugar snap peas and cook for no more than 2 or 3 minutes – they should still have a slight crunch which I like as contrasting texture to the rest of the dish. If you plan to make this ahead, don't add the sugar snap peas till you are going to serve it – don't be tempted to add them initially just to get them included and the whole thing done with!

I like to hand round freshly grated Parmesan cheese with Chickpea and Vegetable Stew.

Pepper and Ham Risotto

Our family, to a man, woman, girl and boy of us, all love both rice and pasta. When there are six in a family it is very often hard to find one thing enthusiastically liked by all, so I suppose I must count myself lucky in this! It opens up vast tracts for supper dishes, and this is one of them.

Risotto needs risotto rice – there is no way you can make risotto using long or short grain rice, you need Arborio or risotto rice, which is a short, almost round grain, with the ability to absorb liquid without becoming mush and somehow retain its shape. It is important to cook the rice in the hot olive oil so that each grain is coated in oil before adding the liquid. And the liquid, which should be the best stock, must be added in small amounts at a time, stirred gently and occasionally as the liquid is absorbed before more is added.

I serve a bowl of freshly grated Parmesan cheese separately. All you need to accompany any risotto is a salad.

SERVES 6

3 red or yellow (or both) peppers	*½ pt/285 ml dry white wine*
4 tbsp olive oil + 2 oz/56 g butter	*2½ pts/1.42 L good chicken stock – the better the stock, the better the risotto will be*
2 onions, skinned and finely chopped	
1 lb/450 g Arborio or risotto rice	*8 oz/225 g smoked ham, trimmed of fat and cut into small bits as neatly as possible*
1–2 cloves of garlic, skinned and finely chopped	*Salt and plenty of freshly ground black pepper*

First, prepare the peppers by cutting each in half and scooping away the seeds. Put the halved peppers skin uppermost on to a baking tray under a hot grill. Grill them till their skins bubble and char, then put them into a large polythene bag and leave them for 10 minutes. After this peel off their skins, and chop the peppers.

In a large sauté pan, or deep frying pan, or a casserole with a wide base, heat the oil and melt the butter. Add the finely chopped onions and cook them till they are soft and transparent-looking, about 5 minutes. Then add the rice and chopped garlic and cook, stirring, so as to coat the grains of rice with the oil and butter, for about 3–4 minutes. Stir in the white wine over a low to moderate heat, so that the liquid very gently bubbles and, as it becomes absorbed by the rice, pour in a little of the stock, and stir from time to time (with a wooden spoon, never a metal or plastic one for risotto!) before adding more stock. Do this till all the stock is used up, adding the chopped peppers about halfway through.

When all the stock is incorporated, stir in the chopped ham, season with salt and pepper, and serve the risotto as soon as possible.

Curry and Honey Roast Chicken

I love the combination of honey with curry powder. I always put the two ingredients together in the mock *Coronation Chicken* recipe I use. When I was given the following recipe by my sister Liv, I knew it would be good – I could 'taste' it by reading it! It is simplicity itself, has to be done ahead so the chicken breasts can marinate in the mixture, and needs only to be popped into the oven to cook before supper.

I think it is good served with sliced potatoes and onions baked in stock, and with steamed spinach or broccoli. An alternative salad which is delicious with this is sliced fennel with chopped oranges.

SERVES 6

6 tbsp honey	*3 tbsp dry white wine*
4 cloves of garlic, skinned and finely chopped	*6 chicken breasts, with the skin on*
4 tsp medium strength curry powder	

If you are using thick honey, run a hot tap and hold the spoon under the very hot water before spooning the honey from the jar – that way the honey will slip easily off the spoon. Repeat between each spoonful. Put the honey, garlic, curry powder and wine into a saucepan and bring the mixture to simmering point over moderate heat. Simmer gently for 1 minute, then cool.

Put the chicken pieces into a heatproof dish or roasting tin and pour the cooled mixture over them, smearing or brushing it over each. Leave for several hours, then bake in a hot oven, 400°F/

200°C/Gas Mark 6, for 25–30 minutes. If the chicken looks as though it is browning too much for your liking, cover with a piece of greaseproof paper or a butter paper halfway through baking. If you want to make the marinade and cook the chicken immediately, don't bother to cool it before smearing it over the chicken.

Baked Cod (or Hake) Fillets in Parsley, Garlic and Olive Oil Paste with Tomatoes

The basis of this recipe was given to me by my friend Jemima who, with her husband Rupert, runs Borealis, the aromatherapic cosmetic shop in Broadford. For many years they lived in Spain, and she was taught to cook fish like this by a Spanish friend in the hills above Granada where they lived. I have heard that aromatherapy massage should be conducted in silence – of this I am incapable, and Jemima and I natter on about food whenever I indulge myself in one of her brilliant massages – never as frequently as I would like!

SERVES 6

6 good pieces of filleted and skinned firm-fleshed white fish	*¹/₂ pt/285 ml olive oil*
	Salt and freshly ground black pepper
6 large cloves of garlic	*6 tomatoes, skinned and sliced*
About ¹/₂ lb/225 g parsley	

Run your fingers over the fish and feel for any bones, and, with a sharp knife, cut them out. Feeling for bones is a sure way of removing them – even the keenest eyesight can't expect to see the bones. Put the fish into a large, shallow, ovenproof dish.

Put the unskinned cloves of garlic into a saucepan with water and bring to simmering point. Simmer for 1 minute, then drain. With scissors snip off their ends – when you squeeze them the garlic should pop out of the skin and into a food processor. Add the parsley and whiz till the mixture forms a paste, then, still whizzing, add the olive oil drop by drop initially, increasing gradually to a thin trickle. Season with salt and ground black pepper and spread this paste over the surface of the fish.

Lay the skinned tomato slices over the entire surface and bake in a moderate oven, 350°F/180°C/Gas Mark 4, for 20–25 minutes, till the fish flakes.

Baked Chicken in Tomato, Tarragon and Mustard Cream

This recipe is based, flavour-wise, on one given to my sister Liv by another great friend, Mary Hodges, an excellent cook. It is my version, simplicity itself and combining lovely summery flavours. It is an essentially summer dish and so I serve it with scrubbed tiny new potatoes, steamed, then tossed in chopped applemint, and with sliced courgettes sautéed in olive oil with garlic – these accompaniment just round off the other summer tastes I love and go very well with the chicken dish.

SERVES 6

1 lb/450 g tomatoes, skinned	*2 tsp grainy mustard*
3 sprigs of fresh tarragon	*6 chicken breasts, with the skin on*
Salt and ground black pepper	*½ pt/285 ml double cream*

Cut each skinned tomato in half and scoop away the seeds. Put the halved seedless tomatoes into a food processor or blender with the tarragon and whiz till a fairly fine purée. Season with salt and pepper, and whiz in the mustard.

Put the chicken pieces into an ovenproof dish, buttered, and pour the tomatoey mixture over them. Bake in a moderately hot oven, 400°F/200°C/Gas Mark 6, for 25–30 minutes. Stick a knife into the thickest part of the bit of chicken in the middle of the dish (the part to cook least) and check that the juices run clear. If they are pink (which will be distinct from the tomato colour, don't worry), pop the dish back for a further 5 minutes' cooking time.

When the chicken is cooked, take the dish out of the oven and pour the tomatoey liquid into a saucepan, adding the cream and stirring well. Bring to simmering point and simmer gently for 3–5 minutes, check the seasoning and pour this back over the chicken. Serve as soon as possible.

Prosciutto, Chicken and Pasta Salad with Sun-Dried Tomatoes

I used to avoid pasta salads whenever possible, until a couple of years ago when I realized that they could be delicious, both looking and tasting good. What I don't like about pasta salads is their stodge, their often anaemic appearance, and then the fact that some people realize this last fact and try to alleviate it by including chopped raw red and green peppers. Ghastly.

The following pasta salad recipe has evolved over the last eighteen months and meets with approval from all our family. It is important, I think, to cook the pasta in stock, then when it is cooked, to drain it and immediately toss the hot pasta in the dressing. That way it absorbs the tastes of the dressing as it cools. I use small pasta, like the bow or shell shapes – the long tagliatelle or spaghetti is impossible for a salad.

SERVES 6

2–3 oz/56–84 g pasta per person – I allow 2 oz, but if there are large and vastly hungry teenage boys, you might need to increase it

Chicken stock to cook the pasta

4 chicken breasts, poached in water with onion and parsley stalks, cooled, then chopped into small bits

6 slices of prosciutto, cut roughly, with as much of the fat removed as possible

A bunch of chives, snipped

4 pieces of sun-dried tomato, drained of their oil and chopped

About 12 black olives, the best, preserved with herbs in oil, stoned and chopped – leave them out if you don't like olives

4 oz sugar snap peas, sliced thinly on the diagonal – these provide a good crunch as well as colour

For the dressing:

1 tsp grainy mustard

$\frac{1}{2}$ tsp salt and plenty of ground black pepper

4 tbsp olive oil

1 tbsp wine vinegar – I don't think it matters whether you use white or red

---

Cook the pasta in plenty of boiling chicken stock till the pasta is al dente. The best way to test for this is to stick your – clean! – nail through a bit. It should feel tender but not soft. Drain and toss in the dressing, which you will need to have ready – just mix all the ingredients together.

As the pasta cools, mix it with all the other salad ingredients. Pile the salad on an ashet or serving plate, and surround it with lettuce leaves and salad greens.

Diced Fish Marinated in Fromage Frais with Herbs

This is a perfect supper for a hot summer's evening. It has to be prepared several hours in advance, so you can get it ready in the morning for supper. I like to serve it with either warm granary bread or Black Olive, Sun-Dried Tomato and Garlic Bread (see page 72). It needs only mixed green salad leaves as an accompaniment apart from the bread.

Use any fish you like, but it is important to have the smoked fish as half the fish quantity. Feel with your fingers for bones, and cut them out with a very sharp knife. This is the only sure way to discover all the bones.

SERVES 6

1 1b/450 g each smoked haddock and firm-fleshed white fish such as cod, hake, or monkfish	*1 tsp sugar*
	½ pinch of salt – the smoked haddock is quite salty
½ pt/285 ml creamy fromage frais	*Plenty of ground black or white pepper*
1 tbsp lemon juice	*4 tbsp chopped dill weed*

With a very sharp knife, slice the fish, both smoked and unsmoked, into small dice, about ¼ inch/½ cm in size. Put the diced fish on to an ashet or large serving plate.

Mix together the fromage frais, lemon juice, sugar, salt, pepper and dill weed, and spread this over the fish, stirring it all up. Leave for several hours, at least six, and stir it up once or twice in that time. Serve.

Scallop and Leek Salad

This is the simplest supper dish, if a rather special one. The tastes of the leeks and scallops go so very well together. The sliced leeks are cooked with a very small amount of chopped fresh ginger in butter and sunflower oil, then the sliced scallops are added to the frying pan. After a brief cooking the contents of the frying pan are dished into a serving dish and a fromage frais based sauce is spooned over, and the leeks and scallops left to cool.

It can be made in the morning for supper that evening, and needs only warm bread, white or granary, and salad to accompany it. You can, if you like, substitute chopped monkfish for the scallops.

SERVES 6

---

18 large scallops
2 oz/56 g butter + tbsp
   sunflower oil
6 medium to large (but
   not woody) leeks,
   washed, trimmed, and
   sliced thinly on the
   diagonal
A 1-in/2.5-cm piece fresh
   root ginger, pared of

its skin and finely
   chopped
1/2 pt/56 g fromage frais
1/2 tsp salt and plenty of
   freshly ground black
   pepper
1 tbsp lemon juice
1 tbsp each snipped chives
   and finely chopped
   parsley

Slice the scallops, each into about three. In a large sauté or frying pan, melt the butter and heat the oil together and cook the sliced leeks over a gentle heat, with the chopped ginger, for about 5–7 minutes – till the leeks feel tender. The ginger will lose its ferocity as it cooks. Then add the sliced scallops and cook them, stirring them around, raising the heat under the pan to moderate. When the slices of scallop turn opaque, 3–4 minutes at the most, scoop the contents of the pan into a serving dish.

Mix together the fromage frais, salt, pepper and lemon juice, and pour this over the leek and scallops mixture. Scatter the chives and parsley over the surface. Leave to cool completely, then serve.

Tomato and Basil Mould with Egg, Feta cheese and Crispy Bacon

This simple tomato and basil flavoured jelly, flecked with chives and parsley, looks nicest made in a ring mould with the hardboiled egg, crispy bacon and small cubes of feta cheese mixture piled in the middle. It needs only warm bread and a good salad to go with it. The tomato mould is best made a day in advance. If the weather is very hot, increase the gelatine by a teaspoonful or two, otherwise the mould will gently collapse under your eyes into a slightly jellied pool around the filling. All the flavours go very well together, and it is perfect summer supper food.

SERVES 6

2 cloves of garlic
1 lb/450 g tomatoes, skinned
A handful of basil
1 tbsp snipped chives
1 tbsp parsley
½ pt/285 ml chicken stock
1½ sachets gelatine (¾ oz/ 21 g)
½ tsp salt and plenty of ground black pepper

For the filling:
6 hardboiled eggs
8 rashers of smoked back bacon, grilled till crisp, then broken into bits
8 oz/225 g feta cheese, sliced into small cubes

Put the garlic cloves into a saucepan with cold water and bring the water to the boil. Simmer for 1 minute, then drain. Snip off the ends of each clove and squeeze the garlic into a food processor – it should pop out of its skins.

Meanwhile, cut each skinned tomato in half and scoop out the seeds. Put the de-seeded tomato halves into the food processor, and add the basil, snipped chives and parsley. Heat the stock and stir in the gelatine, stirring till the granules dissolve completely. Whiz the tomatoes in the processor with the garlic and herbs, and pour in the stock and gelatine. Season with salt and pepper, and pour this mixture into a ring mould about 2 pints/1 litre in size. Leave to set overnight.

Dip the ring mould briefly in warm water – not too hot, if it is a metal mould, otherwise the jelly will melt. Turn the mould on to a serving plate.

Shell and chop the hardboiled eggs. Mix them with the crispy bacon and cubed feta, and spoon this into the middle of the tomatoey mould. Surround with salad leaves, and serve with warm granary bread, or with Black Olive, Sun-Dried Tomato and Garlic Bread (page 72).

Smoked Haddock Roulade with Egg, Cheese and Parsley Filling

Although this roulade has to be made just before supper, it will keep warm satisfactorily for 15–20 minutes. The cheese sauce can be made in the morning and reheated before filling the roulade. All the flavours in this dish complement each other so well – that of the smoked haddock, the hardboiled eggs and sharp cheesy sauce, and the parsley does double duty as both a fresh flavour and a colour 'lifter'.

It is fairly filling, and apart from a salad, and perhaps warm bread, needs no other accompaniment. It is an ideal supper dish either on winter evenings or on a chilly summer's evening, and makes a change from fish pie.

SERVES 6

For the roulade:
1½ lb/675 g smoked (undyed) haddock – or cod
1 onion, skinned
1½ pts/850 ml milk

2 oz/56 g butter
2 oz/56 g flour
Plenty of ground black pepper
A grating of nutmeg
4 large eggs, separated

For the filling:

2 oz/56 g butter

2 oz/56 g flour

¼ pt/140 ml of the smoked haddock milk + ½ pt/285 ml fresh milk

6 hardboiled eggs, shelled and chopped

4 oz/112 g Cheddar cheese, grated

Salt and pepper

2 tbsp finely chopped parsley

Make the roulade by putting the fish into a saucepan with the skinned onion and the 1½ pints/850 ml milk. Slowly bring the milk to a gentle simmer, simmer for 2 minutes, then take the pan off the heat and let the fish cool in the milk. When it is cold, flake the fish, removing all bones and skin, and strain the milk: 1 pint/570 ml into a jug for the roulade, the other ½ pint/285 ml into a separate jug for the filling.

Line a baking tray about 2 inches/5 cm deep with siliconized greaseproof paper (the baking tray measuring about 12 by 15 inches/30 by 37 cm). Melt the butter in a saucepan and stir in the flour. Let it cook for a minute, then gradually add the strained pint/570 ml of fish milk, stirring continuously till the sauce comes to a gentle boil. Take the pan off the heat and season with pepper and nutmeg – the fish will add enough salt for most tastes. Beat in the egg yolks, one by one. Beat in the flaked smoked haddock or smoked cod. In a bowl, whisk the egg whites with a pinch of salt (to give an increased volume) till they are very stiff. With a large metal spoon, fold them quickly and thoroughly through the fishy mixture. Pour this into the paper-lined baking tray and smooth even.

Bake in a moderate oven, 350°F/180°C/Gas Mark 4, till the mixture is firm to the touch, about 25–30 minutes. Take it out of the oven and cover with a damp teatowel for a few minutes before turning it face down on to a work surface lined with baking parchment. Carefully peel the paper off the back of the smoked haddock roulade, tearing it in strips parallel to the surface, to avoid tearing the baked base up with the paper.

Make the sauce by melting the butter in a saucepan and stirring in the flour. Cook for a minute, then gradually add the remainder of the fish milk, and the fresh milk, stirring continuously till the sauce boils. Take the pan off the heat and stir in the chopped eggs, grated cheese, salt and pepper, and lastly the parsley. Spread this filling evenly over the surface of the roulade, and roll it up, rolling away from you, and slipping it on to a large warmed ashet or serving plate. Serve as soon as possible.

Salami, Apple, Celery and New Potato Salad

This is another of those meal-in-one dishes – apart from a few lettuce leaves or bits of salad greenery, it needs no other accompaniment. It's full of complementary tastes and textures, with the crunchiness of the apples and celery, and the garlicy salami – I like to use Milano salami for this, bought in a whole piece rather than sliced, so that I can chop it into small chunks.

It is similar to a recipe in my first book, *Seasonal Cooking*, but I think that it is a definite improvement to add the celery to the original, and to add parsley and chives to the mayonnaise. It all goes to prove the undisputed fact that things go on evolving over the years, and recipes are no exception!

SERVES 6

For the mayonnaise:
1 whole egg + 1 yolk
½ tsp salt
½ tsp sugar
Lots of freshly ground black pepper
½ tsp mustard powder
½ pt/285 ml olive oil – I like to use all olive oil

for this salad rather than a mixture of olive and sunflower oils
2 tbsp wine vinegar (white or red) – add more if you like a sharper flavour to your mayonnaise
1 tbsp snipped chives
1 tbsp chopped parsley

For the salad

1 lb/450g new potatoes, scrubbed, then steamed till just tender

1-lb/450-g piece of Milano salami, rind peeled off, and salami cut into slices about ¹/₂ in/1 cm thick, and then into chunks

6 sticks of celery, washed, trimmed, and sliced diagonally about ¹/₄ in/¹/₂ cm thick

4 good eating apples – not vile and dreary Golden Delicious, but something like Cox's

Start by making the mayonnaise. Put the egg and yolk into a food processor with the salt, sugar, pepper and mustard powder. Whiz, adding the oil drop by drop till you have a good emulsion, then in a thin trickle. Whiz in the vinegar, taste, and add more vinegar if you like a sharper flavour. Whiz in the chives and parsley. If the mayonnaise is very thick, it is rather a good thing for this salad, in my opinion.

Chop the steamed potatoes into large chunks. Put them into a decorative salad bowl with the chopped salami and the sliced celery. Cut each apple into quarters and cut out the cores. Don't skin them, but chop the apples and put them into the bowl with the other salad ingredients. Immediately fold the herby mayonnaise thoroughly into the contents of the bowl. Cover the bowl till you are ready to serve the salad.

Three Bean, Chive and Tomato Salad with Egg Mayonnaise

This is a yummy salad. Luckily all our family love it. I first ate something similar in the Laigh Coffee House in Edinburgh one lunch-time, and thought I could concoct something along the same lines, but without the onion and with some tomato. The chives add enough flavour of the onion family for me, without the rather horrid repetitiveness that raw onion seems to give, and not only to me!

SERVES 6

---

6 tomatoes, skinned
1 lb/450 g fresh broad beans, weighed when shelled, steamed till just tender – the smaller they are, the nicer they will be
A 15-oz/400-g tin of kidney beans, drained of their liquid, rinsed under cold water and patted dry with kitchen paper
³/₄ lb/340 g 'fine' beans, or French beans, cut in 1-in/2.5-cm lengths and steamed till tender – a brief steaming, refresh

under cold water and pat dry
2 tbsp snipped chives
3–4 tbsp French dressing
For the egg mayonnaise:
8 hardboiled eggs, shelled and chopped
6 tbsp good mayonnaise, either bought, or homemade – see the previous recipe for Salami, Apple, Celery and New Potato Salad, and include the chives and parsley or not, as you like

---

Cut each skinned tomato in half and scoop away the seeds. Chop the tomatoes. Mix together the three types of beans, the chives, tomatoes and French dressing – do this several hours before supper if it is more convenient for you. Mix together the chopped eggs and mayonnaise.

Arrange the bean salad around a mound of the egg mayonnaise – it looks more attractive than having two separate bowls. Serve with warm bread and, if you like, with salad leaves.

Spinach, Bacon, Avocado and Feta Cheese Salad

I know that the combination of spinach and avocado is an old one, but if you add chopped crisply cooked bacon, and tiny cubes of feta cheese as well, you have a main course salad which is sustaining to eat as well as being delicious – and very good for you.

All that you need besides this salad is warm bread, either granary bread or the Black Olive Bread on page 72. The quality of spinach to be found in the shops does vary – if you don't grow your own, that is – and I find far and away the best and freshest is always in Marks & Spencer's. Be sparing in the salt in the French dressing for this, or do as I do and just pour good olive oil over the salad, because both the bacon and the feta cheese are quite salty.

SERVES 6

A 2-lb/900-g bag of small spinach leaves, torn into bits (as soon as they are tossed in oil they wilt down)

10 rashers of smoked streaky bacon, grilled till crisp, then broken into bits

4 ripe avocado pears

8 oz/225 g feta cheese, cut into small cubes

Either French dressing, or about 4 tbsp good olive oil

Cut each avocado in half and flick out their stones with the tip of a knife. Slice down their skins and peel them off – this will be easy provided the avocados are ripe – and chop them into cubes. Mix together the avocado, feta, bacon and spinach leaves with either the French dressing or just the olive oil, and serve. Don't dress the salad till just before you eat it, and if you chop the avocados ahead by much more than half an hour, toss them in a tablespoon or two of lemon juice.

Black Olive, Garlic, Parsley and Tomato Pasta

This can't really be described as a sauce, more a collection of things tossed in with the cooked pasta. It is one of our favourite ways of eating pasta – and certainly one of the simplest. We like it best of all with spaghetti, fresh when possible. You do need freshly grated Parmesan cheese to go with it, and good olive oil. And if you buy the really good, juicy black olives which are preserved with herbs, there is a world of difference in comparison with those beastly little stoned black olives which taste of nothing but the brine they are preserved in. If you can only buy that type, it's best to leave them out. If you don't like olives, or can only get the inferior ones, substitute chopped mushrooms, cooked almost to a crisp. The overall taste is different of course, but quite delicious.

SERVES 6

8 tomatoes, skinned	2–3 oz/56–84 g pasta per person
18–20 black olives, stoned and chopped	6 tbsp good extra virgin olive oil
2 large cloves of garlic, skinned and finely chopped	Plenty of ground black pepper
2 large handfuls of parsley, chopped, but not too finely	Fresh Parmesan cheese to hand round separately

Cut each skinned tomato in half and scoop away the seeds. Chop the tomatoes. Mix together the chopped tomatoes, chopped olives, chopped garlic and parsley. Cook the pasta till it is al dente and drain. Immediately measure in the olive oil, stir in the mixed ingredients, add the pepper and serve. If you haven't already got one, a large pasta fork is invaluable for serving cooked pasta.

Red Onion and
Red Pepper Tart with Cheese Pastry

I don't think we use red onions enough in our cooking. They are much more widely available to us these days, and their taste is much milder and really nicer for certain dishes by far than the usual onions. In this tart they are gently fried till soft with the skinned red peppers (they go together very well) and then set with a creamy custard. The cheese and mustard in the pastry just round off the flavours, I think. All else you need to complete this supper dish is a good green salad.

SERVES 6

For the pastry:
5 oz/140 g plain flour
5 oz/140 g butter, hard from the fridge, cut in bits
2 tsp mustard powder
3 oz/84 g Cheddar cheese, grated

For the filling:
2 red peppers
3 tbsp sunflower oil
6 red onions, skinned and very finely sliced
2 whole eggs beaten with 2 large egg yolks
3/4 pt/420 ml single cream
Salt and ground black pepper

Put the flour, butter and mustard powder into a food processor and whiz till the mixture resembles fine crumbs. Then add the Cheddar cheese and whiz very briefly to incorporate it. Pat this firmly around the sides and base of a flan dish measuring approximately 9 inches/23 cm in diameter.

Put the dish into the fridge for an hour before baking, then move it straight from the fridge into a moderate oven, 350°F/180°C/Gas Mark 4, for about 25 minutes, or till the pastry is pale golden. Take it out of the oven.

To make the filling, start by cutting the peppers in half and scooping away their seeds. Put them on a baking tray, skin side uppermost, under a hot grill, and grill till the skin swells into great charred bubbles. Take the peppers out, put them into a polythene bag, and leave for 10 minutes, then skin them. Their skins will peel off easily. Slice the peppers into thin strips.

Heat the oil in a wide-based saucepan and cook the sliced onions over a moderate heat, stirring from time to time so that they don't stick, for about 10 minutes. Then add the sliced peppers and cook for a further 2–3 minutes. Spoon this mixture over the base of the cooked pastry. Mix together the beaten eggs and yolks with the cream, season with salt and pepper, and carefully pour this in with the onions and peppers mixture.

Carefully, so as not to spill the contents, put the flan dish into a moderate oven, 350°F/180°C/Gas Mark 4, till the filling is just set when you gently shake the dish – about 20 minutes.

Serve cold or warm.

Spinach and Goats' Cheese Tart

These flavours go together so well. An optional addition is chopped walnuts – optional because although I think that walnuts and goats' cheese go together as well as do basil and tomatoes, if you don't like walnuts there is no point in adding them. I use a creamy goats' cheese for this, rather than a hard one which needs to be grated.

Like the last recipe, this tart is delicious served cold as well as warm. It is good with a salad of steamed leeks and skinned sliced tomatoes in a French dressing.

For the pastry:
4 oz/112 g butter, hard from the fridge, cut into bits
6 oz/170 g plain flour
1 tsp icing sugar
1/2 tsp salt
Ground black pepper
For the filling:
1 tbsp sunflower oil
2 red onions, skinned and very thinly sliced or finely chopped

1 lb/450 g fresh spinach, steamed till it just wilts, then chopped
3 oz/84 g chopped walnuts – optional
8 oz/225 g goats' cheese
2 large eggs beaten well with 2 large egg yolks
1/2 pt/285 ml single cream
Salt and ground black pepper
A grating of nutmeg

Put all the ingredients for the pastry into a food processor and whiz till the mixture is like fine crumbs. Pat it firmly around the base and sides of a flan dish measuring approximately 9 inches/23 cm in diameter. I use a china flan dish, not the tin ones which are too shallow – I like a good depth to my tarts!

Put the flan dish into the fridge for an hour, and then put it straight into a moderate oven, 350°F/180°C/Gas Mark 4, for about 25 minutes, till the pastry is golden brown. Take the dish out of the oven.

To make the filling, start by heating the oil in a saucepan and cooking the sliced red onions till they are soft and just beginning to turn golden at the edges – about 5 minutes. Then scatter them over the base of the cooked pastry. Scatter the chopped steamed spinach over – and the walnuts, if you are including them. Put the goats' cheese, trimmed of its rind, into a processor, and whiz, gradually adding the beaten eggs and yolks, and the cream. Season with salt, pepper and nutmeg, and pour this carefully over the onions and spinach in the flan case.

Carefully, so as not to spill the contents, put the dish into a moderate oven, 350°F/180°C/Gas Mark 4, till the filling is just firm when you gently shake the dish, about 25–30 minutes.

Serve warm or cold.

Smoked Haddock and Parsley Mousse

This makes a very good main course for supper in warm summer months. (Incidentally, it makes a very good first course at any time of the year.) As with every recipe which calls for smoked haddock, the end result will be the better for the smoked haddock being really plump and juicy – and undyed, it goes without saying. Also, you can substitute smoked cod for the smoked haddock – I love smoked cod, with its great succulent flakes of fish, and these days we can usually choose which we prefer. The parsley flecks the mousse with green, and looks much more interesting than just the plain pale yellow mousse. Looks do matter, and a visually appealing dish will entice the reluctant eater!

It needs only a salad, and warm granary bread as accompaniments.

SERVES 6

2 lb/900 g smoked haddock (or cod)	1 sachet gelatine (½ oz/14 g)
2 pts/1.1 L milk and water mixed	6 tbsp mayonnaise
1 onion, skinned and cut in half	¼ pt/140 ml fromage frais
	Plenty of ground black pepper
2 sticks of celery, washed and broken in half	3 tbsp finely chopped parsley
	2 egg whites

Put the fish into a large saucepan with the milk and water and the onion and celery. Put the pan over a moderate heat and heat till the liquid just begins to heave under a skin, then take the pan off the heat, and leave to get completely cold.

Measure ¼ pint/140 of the liquid the fish cooked in into a small saucepan, and sprinkle in the gelatine. Warm – take care not to let it boil – till the gelatine granules dissolve completely.

Flake the fish, removing all bones and skin. Mix together the mayonnaise and fromage frais, stir in the cooled gelatine mixture and season with pepper. Fold in the flaked fish and the chopped parsley. Lastly, whisk the egg whites in a bowl till they are stiff, then, with a large metal spoon, fold them quickly and thoroughly through the fish mixture.

Scrape the mousse into a serving bowl, cover, and leave in the fridge till you want to serve it. This can be made a day in advance.

Vegetable and Cheese Millefeuille

Now that we can buy ready rolled out sheets of puff pastry, I have found a wide variety of recipes that I can experiment with. I loathe rolling out pastry, and make such a bad job of it, and these ready rolled out sheets of puff pastry really are a boon for people like me. They bake evenly – you can cut them, before baking them, into neat oblongs, brush them with beaten egg and bake them. I like to scatter various things on them, in this recipe grated cheese mixed with paprika. In a sweet recipe, once the millefeuille cases are baked I like to sieve icing sugar over the insides, finely grate lemon rind over it, and put them under a hot grill to caramelize. They make a change from potatoes, rice and pasta, and people of all ages seem to love puff pastry – most gratifying!

In this recipe you can use whichever vegetables you have to hand. There really is no need for any other accompaniment except, perhaps, a salad.

SERVES 6

About 2 lb/900 g ready rolled out puff pastry	For the filling:
1 large egg, beaten	*2 oz/56 g butter*
4 oz/112 g Cheddar cheese, finely grated	*2 tbsp sunflower oil*
1 tbsp paprika	*2 onions, finely chopped*
	2 sticks of celery, washed, trimmed and finely sliced

½ lb/225 g mushrooms, wiped, stalks cut level with the caps, and chopped	*A grating of nutmeg*
	About ½ lb/225 g broccoli, trimmed into florets and the pieces of stem (which I love) trimmed into matchsticks, and both steamed till barely tender
2 oz/56 g flour	
1¼ pts/710 ml milk	
1 clove of garlic, skinned and finely chopped	
4 oz/112 g Cheddar cheese, grated	
Salt and ground black pepper	*1 medium cauliflower, trimmed into small florets, and steamed till just tender*

Brush the pieces of raw puff pastry with beaten egg, then gently press the cheese on to each, just a scattering. Scatter a small amount of paprika over the cheese and bake in a hot oven, 420°F/220°C/Gas Mark 7, till well puffed up and dark golden. Take them out of the oven, and carefully split each one in two. Put them on a plate or rack to keep warm, keeping the cheese bits on one side and the plain bits, for the bases, on the other.

Make the vegetable filling by melting the butter and heating the oil in a large saucepan. Add the chopped onions and sliced celery and cook, stirring occasionally, till the onions are transparent and beginning to turn golden at the edges, and the celery is soft. Stir in the mushrooms, and cook for a minute or two before stirring in the flour. Let this cook for a minute, then add the milk gradually, stirring continuously till the sauce boils. Add the chopped garlic now. This will give a good garlic flavour – if you add it with the onions, it loses its flavour the longer it cooks. Take the pan off the heat, stir in the grated cheese, season with salt, pepper and nutmeg, and fold in the steamed broccoli and cauliflower bits.

To serve, warm up the puff pastry, put two bases on each warmed plate, and divide the vegetable filling between the puff pastry bases. Cover each with its cheese-topped 'lid', and serve.

Meatballs with Tomato sauce and Spinach Purée

These are so convenient because they can be made completely in advanced and reheated in their tomato sauce. They are nicest, I think, served with puréed spinach. The spinach, too, reheats without deteriorating in taste or texture.

Just as it is, this is a good supper, but if you have hungry children, baked jacket potatoes go very well with the meatballs. If you are making this dish in the summer, substitute new potatoes, steamed in their skins, for the baked potatoes.

SERVES 6

For the meatballs:

1¹/₂ lb/675 g rump steak, trimmed of fat and gristle

1 lb/450 g good pork sausages, made with a high percentage of porkmeat as opposed to the odds and ends of the animal

1 tbsp sunflower or olive oil

1 onion, skinned and chopped as finely as possible

3 tbsp flour sieved with plenty of ground black pepper

Sunflower oil for frying the meatballs

For the tomato sauce:

3 tbsp olive oil

2 onions, skinned and finely chopped

2 sticks of celery, washed, trimmed and finely sliced

1–2 cloves of garlic, skinned and finely chopped

Two 15-oz/420-g tins of chopped tomatoes

1 tsp pesto (the basil sauce)

¹/₂ tsp salt and ground black pepper

For the spinach purée:

4 lb/1.8 kg fresh spinach, steamed till it wilts, just

8 oz/225 g Philadelphia cream cheese, or reduced fat equivalent (Shape or Light)

Salt and pepper

A grating of nutmeg

Start by making the meatballs. Cut the trimmed meat in chunks and put them into the food processor. With a sharp knife, slit down each sausage skin; it will then slip off the sausage easily. Put the skinned sausages into the processor. Heat the oil in a saucepan and add the very finely chopped onion. Cook for 3–4 minutes, then put it into the processor. Whiz, till the mixture is well mixed but not a complete mush.

Flour your hands and form the meaty mixture into small balls, as even in size as possible. Roll them in the seasoned flour. Put them on a foil-lined tray or large plate. Cover them and keep them in the fridge till you want to cook them.

To cook them, heat some sunflower oil in a wide frying pan or similar, and fry the meatballs, turning them over so that they brown on all sides. Remove them to a warm serving dish.

Make the tomato sauce by heating the olive oil in a saucepan and adding the chopped onions and sliced celery. Cook, stirring occasionally, till the onion is really soft, and beginning to go golden, then stir in the garlic, chopped tomatoes, pesto, salt and pepper. Simmer the sauce very gently for 20 minutes. Either serve it as it is, slightly chunkily textured, or liquidize it for a velvety smooth sauce.

Whiz the steamed spinach in a processor with the cream cheese, salt, pepper and nutmeg.

To serve, pour the tomato sauce over the meatballs and reheat gently. Put the spinach into a low temperature oven for 20–25 minutes to reheat. Serve each person a spoonful of the spinach purée with the meatballs in their tomato sauce on top.

Casseroled Pork with Vegetables and Soya Sauce

Pork doesn't need as long to cook as do meats like beef, lamb and venison. But it makes casseroles which can be eaten as suitably in the summer as in the winter, whereas beef-based casseroles and stews really are for winter eating.

In this recipe the pork is cooked with vegetables and seasoned with soya sauce. Now, soya sauce varies considerably from make to make. There is usually a choice available to us on most supermarket shelves, not only of different brands of soya sauce (incidentally, I like the one called 'Superior Soy' best), but you will notice there are two strengths – 'light', and 'dark', which is also sometimes called 'strong'. The light is meant for use with fish and chicken and light meats such as pork, the dark with more robust meats like beef and venison. But I don't think the light is worth buying – I use the stronger one always. The light tastes dilute.

I like to serve boiled Basmati rice with this casserole, and a green vegetable like sautéed courgettes with garlic.

Serves 6

3 tbsp sunflower oil	3 carrots, peeled, trimmed and sliced into very thin matchsticks
2 onions, skinned and finely sliced	
1–2 cloves of garlic, skinned and finely chopped	2 lb/900 g pork, cut into cube-shaped 1-in/2.5-cm pieces
3 medium leeks, washed, trimmed and finely sliced	1 tbsp flour
	1 pt/570 ml vegetable or chicken stock
3 sticks of celery, washed, trimmed and finely sliced	3 tbsp strong soya sauce
	Salt and ground black pepper

Heat the oil in a casserole and add the onions. Cook them, stirring from time to time to prevent them from sticking, till they are transparent-looking and beginning to turn golden at the edges. Then add the garlic and other prepared vegetables and cook them, stirring occasionally, for about 5 minutes. Scoop them out and into a warm bowl, draining as much oil as you can back into the casserole.

Brown the cut-up pork, a small amount at a time, removing it to the bowl with the vegetables as it browns. Stir in the flour, cook for a minute, then, stirring continuous, add the stock, stirring till the sauce bubbles. Stir in the soya sauce and the salt and pepper, and replace the meat and vegetables in the casserole.

Put the lid on and cook in a moderate oven, 350°F/180°C/Gas Mark 4, for 45 minutes. If you make it in advance, cool it completely before storing it in the fridge. Before reheating, take the casserole from the fridge and into room temperature for an hour, then reheat it in a moderate oven for 20–25 minutes.

Pork Chops with Apples, Onions and Cider

This is another quick, useful and delicious supper dish. I like to serve it with creamily mashed potatoes and a green leafy vegetable such as cabbage, or Brussels sprouts if they are in season.

SERVES 6

3 tbsp sunflower oil

6 pork chops, trimmed of excess fat

2 onions, skinned and finely sliced (or chopped, if you prefer)

1 clove of garlic, skinned and finely chopped

1 heaped tbsp flour

1 pt/570 ml dry cider – or unsweetened apple juice, if you prefer

3 good eating apples, such as Granny Smith's, or Cox's if they are in season, peeled, quartered, cored and thinly sliced

Salt and freshly ground black pepper

Heat the oil in a wide shallow pan and brown the chops on each side. Put them into an ovenproof dish.

Add the sliced onions to the pan and cook them gently, stirring occasionally, till they are soft and just beginning to turn transparent. Stir in the chopped garlic, cook for a minute, then stir in the flour. Stirring all the time, gradually add the cider, and let the sauce come to boiling point. Add the sliced apples, and season with salt and pepper. Pour this sauce over the chops.

Cover the dish with either a lid or foil, and bake in a moderate oven, 350°F/180°C/Gas Mark 4, for 25–30 minutes. If you bake the dish from cold, having got it to that stage several hours in advance, allow an extra 10 minutes for cooking.

Ham Terrine

This is delicious and any left-over can be served cold, but it is very good hot, with creamy mashed potatoes into which I like to beat chopped parsley and snipped chives, and with broad beans in a parsley sauce. It is so simple to make, but you can't make it in advance and reheat it; you can, on the other hand, prepare it in the morning all ready to bake before supper, so you can get the washing up done well ahead!

SERVES 6

1 lb/450 g good pork sausages	*¼ tsp ground cinnamon*
1½ lb/675 g roast or boiled ham	*A pinch of ground cloves*
Lots of ground black pepper – no salt will be needed	*2 large eggs beaten with ½ pt/285 ml single cream*

Line the base and short ends of a 2-lb/900-g loaf tin with baking parchment.

Slit the sausages with a sharp knife and put the sausagemeat into a food processor. Cut up the ham, removing all fat, and put this, too, in the processor. Add the pepper, cinnamon and cloves and whiz, gradually pouring in the beaten eggs and cream mixture. Scrape this into the prepared tin, cover the top with a strip of baking parchment (which prevents the top developing a crisp crust), and put the loaf tin in a roasting tin with water coming halfway up the sides.

Bake in a moderate oven, 350°F/180°C/Gas Mark 4, for 1½–1¾ hours. Turn out and slice to serve. If you like, the tomato sauce in the meatballs recipe (page 233) is very good with this Ham Terrine.

Braised Brisket with Root Vegetables

Brisket is a fatty cut of meat, cut from the breast of the animal. It needs to be braised or pot roasted, cooled, and when cold the fat skimmed from the surface. But it has a very good flavour, and makes a really good supper main course, especially when braised with a variety of root vegetables, as in this recipe.

It needs only baked potatoes as an accompaniment, and any left-over can either be taken out of the vegetables and sliced, and served cold, or reheated in the vegetables. If you serve it cold, you can whiz the remains of the vegetables into soup.

This may sound a lot for six, but the meat shrinks dramatically during cooking.

SERVES 6

2 tbsp sunflower oil	3 carrots, peeled and chopped
4 lb/1.8 kg brisket, boned and rolled, which is how it is usually bought	3 parsnips, peeled and chopped
3 onions, skinned and chopped	½ medium to small turnip, skin cut off and chopped
3 leeks, washed, trimmed and sliced	

4 sticks of celery, washed, trimmed and sliced	*1 can lager*
2 tbsp tomato purée	*1 pt/570 ml water*
2 tbsp flour	*Salt and ground black pepper*

You will see, when you have prepared the vegetables, that it looks rather a large amount. Don't worry – they, like the meat, go down by about half during cooking time. But you do need a fairly large casserole to cook this in.

Heat the oil in the casserole and brown the meat all over. Take it out of the casserole and put it on a warm dish. Add the onions to the casserole and cook them, stirring occasionally, till they are transparent, then add the rest of the vegetables. Cook them, stirring from time to time, for about 10 minutes then stir in the tomato purée and the flour. Cook for a minute then stir in the lager and the water, stirring till bubbles appear. Replace the meat, pushing it down amongst the vegetables, season with salt and pepper and put the lid on the casserole.

Cook in a slow to moderate oven, 300°F/150°C/Gas Mark 3, for 2 hours, then take the casserole out of the oven, let it cool completely and store it in the fridge. Before serving, take it out of the fridge and into room temperature for an hour before putting it back into an oven, at a moderate temperature this time, 350°F/180°C/Gas Mark 4, for a further 1½ hours' cooking. Before replacing it in the oven, skim any fat from the surface.

To serve, lift the meat on to a board, cut away the string, and slice the meat, spooning the vegetables and the juices around.

Casseroled Beef with Mushrooms and Black Olives

As with every recipe which calls for black olives, this one needs the very best black olives, those preserved with herbs and not the black olives preserved in brine, which impart a very strong and not

altogether pleasant flavour to this or any other dish for that matter.
This casserole has rather Mediterranean flavours, and is delicious. I
like to serve it with creamy mashed potatoes, and with a green
vegetable, or with a salad. As with virtually all casseroles, it benefits
from being made in advance and reheated – somehow the flavours
seem to mingle better than eating it after its initial cooking.

SERVES 6

2 lb/900 g stewing beef, or rump, trimmed and cut into 1 in/2.5 cm bits	*¹/₂ lb/225 g mushrooms, wiped and chopped*
2 tbsp flour sieved with ¹/₂ tsp salt and lots of ground black pepper	*1–2 cloves of garlic, skinned and finely chopped*
4 tbsp olive oil	*1 tbsp tomato purée*
2 onions, skinned and finely sliced	*³/₄ pt/420 ml water*
	¹/₂ pt/285 ml red wine
	About 12 black olives, stones removed and olives chopped

Toss the cut-up meat in the seasoned flour. Heat the olive oil in a
heavy casserole and brown the meat, a little at a time. Remove the
browned meat to a warm dish. Next, lower the heat a bit and add the
onions, cooking them till they are transparent – about 5 minutes.
Scoop them into the dish with the meat and raise the heat under the
casserole. Fry the chopped mushrooms almost till they are crisp – this
greatly improves their flavour. Lower the heat again, and add the
chopped garlic, the olives, the tomato purée, and, stirring all the
time, the wine and water. Replace the onions and meat.

Put a lid on the casserole, and cook it in a moderate oven, 350°F/
180°C/Gas Mark 4, for 1¼ hours. Take it out of the oven, cool
completely, and store it in the fridge. Before reheating, take the
casserole out of the fridge and into room temperature for an hour,
then reheat in a moderate oven for 30 minutes. The sauce should be
gently simmering around the meat.

Pork Chops with Onions and Oranges

This dish has the fruity flavour of the orange which goes so well with pork. It can be made a day in advance, if it is more convenient for you, and reheated before serving. I like to serve it with either new potatoes with mint, or creamy mashed potatoes, and with a green vegetable – sugar snap peas stir-fried with ginger and garlic are especially good with this. But so is steamed broccoli, or Brussels sprouts.

SERVES 6

3 tbsp sunflower oil	*½ pt/285 ml fresh orange juice*
6 loin, or sometimes called chump, chops	*1 pt/570 ml chicken stock*
3 onions, skinned and finely chopped	*Juice of ½ lemon*
1 tbsp flour	*Salt and pepper*
	3 oranges, skin cut off and cut into segments

Heat the oil and briefly seal the trimmed chops on each side. Put them into a warmed dish and add the chopped onions to the oil. Cook them till they turn soft and transparent, about 5 minutes, then stir in the flour. Cook for a minute, then gradually stir in the orange juice, stock and lemon juice, stirring till the sauce boils. Put the chops back into the sauce, pushing them down and covering them with the orangey onion sauce.

Cover with a lid, and bake in a moderate oven, 350°F/180°C/Gas Mark 4, for 30 minutes. Taste, season with salt and pepper, and just before serving, stir the orange segments into the casserole contents.

Sausagemeat Puffed Pastry Plate Pie

This is one of those top-and-bottom pies which is delicious eaten hot or cold. Now that we can buy ready rolled out puff pastry, making something like this takes minutes. Because the pie is cooked in a metal deep plate shape it means that you will need two plate pies in order to feed the average appetites of a growing family. The sausagemeat you use depends on your tastes – if you prefer beef sausages, substitute them for the pork ones. The better the sausages, the better will be the end result.

SERVES 6

One 1 lb/450 g packet of ready rolled out puff pastry	1 tsp medium strength curry powder
2 oz/56 g butter	2 lb/900 g good pork sausages
2 onions, skinned and finely chopped	6 tomatoes, skinned, cut in half and seeds thrown away, and chopped
1 clove of garlic, skinned and finely chopped	Ground black pepper – no salt needed
	1 egg, beaten

Cut four circles of pastry, marking around one of your metal pie plates. Put one circle of pastry on each of two plates.

Melt the butter in a saucepan and add the chopped onions. Cook for several minutes, till the onions are soft, then add the chopped garlic, and the curry powder. Cook for a minute, then cool this mixture. Slit down each sausage with a sharp knife and peel off the skins. Put the sausages into a bowl, and add the chopped tomatoes, the pepper and the cooled onion mixture. With your hand, mix all together thoroughly.

Divide this mixture between each pastry-lined plate, and press down to cover the bases. Cover with the remaining circles of pastry, and crimp the edges together. Brush each with beaten egg, slash three or four times in the tops to let any steam out during cooking, and bake in a hot oven, 400°F/200°C/Gas Mark 6, till the pastry is golden and puffed up, about 25 minutes, then lower the temperature to moderate, 350°F/180°C/Gas Mark 4, and cook for a further 15 minutes. If the tops of the pies look as if they are becoming too brown for your liking, cover each with a piece of baking parchment.

Serve hot or cold

Cheese and Tomato Pudding

For this old-fashioned but nonetheless delicious supper dish, it is vital to use baked bread, not steamed sliced. If you don't like tomatoes, just leave them out, but I think they 'make' this. I like to serve a good herb-filled green salad as an accompaniment. You can mix the egg yolks, milk and cream in the morning, and grate the cheese, ready to assemble and bake before supper.

SERVES 6

Six 1-in/2.5-cm thick slices baked white bread, crusts cut off and slices cut in half

1 pt/570 ml milk, or ½ pt/ 285 ml milk and ½ pt/285 ml single cream

2 cloves of garlic, poached for 1 minute, then squeezed out of their skins

and pounded with 1 tsp mustard powder

3 large whole eggs + 1 large egg yolk

6 oz/170 g Cheddar cheese, grated

6 tomatoes, skinned, de- seeded and chopped

Salt and ground black pepper

Butter a large ovenproof dish. Arrange the slices of bread in it. Mix a small amount of the milk or milk and cream with the garlic and mustard powder mixture, then mix it in with the rest of the milk.

Beat together the eggs and yolk, and then beat together the eggs
and milk and garlic mustard mixture. Scatter the grated cheese
over the bread, and then scatter the chopped tomatoes over. Pour
the milk and eggs over the lot, and season with salt and pepper.

Bake in a moderate oven, 350°F/180°C/Gas Mark 4, till the
custard is just set, about 25 minutes. Serve as soon as you can.

Broccoli and Mushroom Risotto

Mushroom Risotto is my great stand-by when I am racking my
brain about what to have for supper. I always keep a large supply of
Arborio rice (the rice with which risotto is made) in my storecupboard, and if you have good chicken (or vegetable) stock to hand,
with just a handful of vegetables you can make a delicious supper,
needing only a salad as accompaniment. Mushrooms, I think, make
the best risotto, but the other day I had a head of broccoli and I
used that with the mushrooms. It was voted a winning combination, and I've made it twice since that first time. Freshly grated
Parmesan cheese is an essential, to be handed around for your
supper eaters to help themselves.

SERVES 6

4–5 tbsp olive oil
2 onions, skinned and finely
    chopped
1½ lb/675 g broccoli
2–3 oz/56–84 g Arborio rice
    per person (3 oz for
    younger ones, 2 for
    older)

1–2 cloves of garlic,
    skinned and very finely
    chopped
1 lb/450 g mushrooms,
    wiped and chopped
3 pts/1.7 L chicken stock
¼ pt/140 ml dry white
    wine
Salt and freshly ground
    black pepper

Heat the oil in a large sauté pan and cook the onions till they are soft. Meanwhile, trim the broccoli into small florets, and slice the stems into neat matchsticks. Add the rice and garlic to the onions in the pan, and the mushrooms, and cook for about 4–5 minutes, stirring, so that each grain of rice is coated in oil. Then add the broccoli and, a small amount at a time, the stock and wine, stirring occasionally, and cooking over a low to moderate heat. Cook like this till all the stock is incorporated. Season with salt and black pepper, and serve – it shouldn't be stodgy, but fairly sloppy.

Chicken Stew with Parsley and Chive Dumplings

This is one of those dishes which you think of longingly when on an endless cold and wet walk. It's the sort of dish which conjures up the image in your mind of an appreciative family sniffing in anticipation as the mother lifts the lid from the casserole! My family is never that idyllic – I am usually yelling at them that supper is ready and to hurry up!

The dumplings make any other starch unnecessary, but because of the root vegetables in the stew I do like to serve a green vegetable as accompaniment.

SERVES 6

1 chicken, about 3¹/₂ lb/1.6 kg
2 onions, skinned and cut in half
2 leeks, washed and chopped
¹/₂ tsp rock salt
A handful of peppercorns

For the stew:
2 oz/56 g butter + 2 tbsp sunflower oil
2 onions, skinned and finely chopped
3 carrots, peeled and chopped
4 medium leeks, washed, trimmed and sliced

4 sticks of celery, washed,
   trimmed and sliced
4 parsnips, peeled and
   chopped
½ medium turnip, peeled
   and chopped
2 tbsp flour
2 pts/1.1 L chicken stock
Salt and ground black
   pepper

For the dumplings;
1 tbsp sunflower oil
1 onion, skinned and very
   finely chopped
12 oz/340 g self-raising
   flour sieved with ½ tsp
   salt and ground black
   pepper
1 tbsp each chopped
   parsley and snipped
   chives
3 tbsp grated suet
½ pt/285 ml milk

Put the chicken into a saucepan with the first lot of onions and leeks, and the rock salt and peppercorns. Cover with water, bring to simmering point, then cover with a lid and simmer gently for 1 hour. Stick a knife into the chicken's thigh – if the juices run clear, the chicken is cooked; if they are even slightly tinged with pink, continue to simmer for a further 5 or 10 minutes.

Take the pan off the heat and let the chicken cool in the liquid. Then lift it out and cut all the meat from the carcase. Replace the carcase in the stock and boil gently, pan uncovered, for 45 minutes. Strain.

To make the stew, melt the butter and heat the oil together in a large casserole. Add the chopped onions and cook them till they turn soft and transparent-looking, then stir in the other vegetables and cook, stirring from time to time, for about 10 minutes. Stir in the flour, cook for a minute, then add the stock, stirring all the time till the mixture comes to boiling point. Season with salt and pepper.

Cover with a lid and cook in a moderate oven, 350°F/180°C/Gas Mark 4, for 35–40 minutes. The vegetables should be soft when you stick a fork into them – try a piece of carrot, they take the longest to cook.

To make the dumplings, heat the sunflower oil and cook the very finely chopped onion in it till soft. Cool, then mix well with the seasoned flour, herbs and suet, and then mix in the milk to bind it all together.

In a saucepan of fast-boiling water or stock, cook spoonfuls of this mixture – they swell during cooking – for 10 minutes each. Lift them out with a slotted spoon, and put them into the vegetable stew. Carefully stir in the chicken, and reheat till the whole stew simmers gently for about 10 minutes. Serve.

Index

INDEX

THE CLAIRE MACDONALD COOKBOOK
by Claire Macdonald of Macdonald

Clarissa Dickson Wright, now famous for her role in *Two Fat Ladies*, has described Kinloch Lodge on the Isle of Skye as 'the hotel where Claire Macdonald and her husband Godfrey cheerfully dispense peace, good humour and wonderful food'. Distilled from Claire's years of cooking at Kinloch Lodge, this is a celebratory collection of the best of the recipes from her many books together with much new material.

Revised and updated to take account of the health- and weight-conscious Nineties, the recipes range exhaustively across soups, first courses, fish, poultry and game, meat, eggs, vegetables (both as a main course and a side dish), salads, pasta and rice, stocks, sauces and a selection of delicious breads, cakes and puddings in every shape and form.

Claire Macdonald, whose hallmarks are the use of seasonal, fresh country ingredients, and practical, down-to-earth methods, is justly renowned for her cookery writing. Whether providing ideas for informal family fare, intimate gourmet meals or special occasion dishes, Claire is a remarkably reliable source of foolproof and marvellous recipes. *The Claire Macdonald Cookbook* is an indispensable addition to every cook's *batterie de cuisine*.

0 593 04268 9

NOW AVAILABLE AS A BANTAM PRESS HARDBACK

SEASONAL COOKING
by Claire Macdonald of Macdonald

'Inspires confidence while whetting the taste buds'
Jocasta Innes, *Sunday Times*

On the Isle of Skye, Claire Macdonald, with her husband, is famous for her cooking at Kinloch Lodge where the Macdonalds entertain their family, friends and guests.

This book is a distillation of her years of cooking on Skye and the 200 recipes are a combination of family food and gourmet dishes which blend the use of seasonal ingredients with her own special talent for serving delicious fare.

There are homely soups, pot roasts, pies and puddings juxta-posed with tempting specialities like Chicken and Broccoli in Mayonnaise Cream Sauce; Mushroom, Cheese and Garlic Soufflé and sensational desserts such as Raspberries with Cinnamon Ice Cream or inspirational first courses of Stilton Stuffed Pancakes with Tomato Sauce.

Seasonal Cooking is a marvellous invitation to enjoy fresh country flavours and a first-class source for every ambitious cook.

'. . . wholesome and imaginative cookery'
House & Garden

0 552 99216 X

CELEBRATIONS
by Claire Macdonald of Macdonald

Celebrations is written for anyone who likes to eat and drink well, and to celebrate the milestones in their lives. Almost any event can be an excuse for a party or a feast — birthdays, Christmas, anniversaries, christenings, or even just a summer party or barbecue — and Claire Macdonald, who runs a family hotel at Kinloch Lodge on the Isle of Skye, offers a host of delicious recipes to help even the most hard-pressed cook celebrate life.

Menus range from romantic dinners for two to lunch or dinner parties for twenty or more. *Celebrations* also includes a stunning selection of the puddings for which Claire Macdonald is so justly famous.

Above all, the recipes are supremely practical and many can be prepared in advance; *Celebrations* is aimed at those of us who love to entertain but have to cope with busy lives as well.

'Claire Macdonald of Macdonald is plainly one of nature's hostesses . . . the recipes are many of them novel as well as practical'
Glasgow Herald

0 552 99436 7

OTHER CLAIRE MACDONALD COOKERY TITLES
AVAILABLE FROM CORGI BOOKS AND BANTAM PRESS

THE PRICES SHOWN BELOW WERE CORRECT AT THE TIME OF GOING TO PRESS. HOWEVER TRANSWORLD PUBLISHERS RESERVE THE RIGHT TO SHOW NEW RETAIL PRICES ON COVERS WHICH MAY DIFFER FROM THOSE PREVIOUSLY ADVERTISED IN THE TEXT OR ELSEWHERE.

☐ 99216 X	**SEASONAL COOKING**	£6.99
☐ 99288 7	**MORE SEASONAL COOKING**	£6.99
☐ 99436 7	**CELEBRATIONS**	£7.99
☐ 99217 8	**SWEET THINGS**	£6.99
☐ 14428 2	**LUNCHES**	£6.99
☐ 04268 9	**THE CLAIRE MACDONALD COOKBOOK** (Hardback)	£25.00

All Transworld titles are available by post from:
Bookpost, P.O. Box 29, Douglas, Isle of Man IM99 1BQ

Credit cards accepted. Please telephone 01624 836000,
fax 01624 837033, Internet http://www.bookpost.co.uk or
e-mail: bookshop@enterprise.net for details.

Free postage and packing in the UK. Overseas customers allow
£1 per book (paperbacks) and £3 per book (hardbacks).